# Power of Prayer

## Ellen G. White

**TEACH Services, Inc.**
P U B L I S H I N G
*www.TEACHServices.com*

---

Copyright © 1994, 2011 TEACH Services, Inc.
ISBN-13: 978-1-57258-002-2 (Paperback)
ISBN-13: 978-1-57258-950-6 (ePub)
ISBN-13: 978-1-57258-754-0 (Kindle/Mobi)
Library of Congress Control Number: 94-78149

*Published by*

**TEACH Services, Inc.**
P U B L I S H I N G
*www.TEACHServices.com*

# Introduction

What is more important in this life than prayer? Prayer is our connection with God—our strength, our bridge to heaven!

It is when "men begin to call upon the name of the Lord" that they find him (Gen. 4:26). We are told that He "hearest prayer" (Ps. 65:2). What a promise that is! As we pray, the Holy Spirit Himself unites in our petitions and "maketh intercession for us" (Rom. 8:26, 27). We are not alone in the battle of life; all heaven is on our side!

And how many are the promises for us to persevere! "Seek the Lord and His strength, seek His face continually" (1 Chron. 16:11). "Watch and pray that ye enter not into temptation" (Matt. 26:41). "Hitherto have ye asked nothing in My name: ask, and ye shall receive, that your joy may be full" (John 16:24). "Ask, and it shall be given you: seek, and ye shall find; knock, and it shall be opened unto you" (Matt. 7:7).

"And the Lord said unto him, I have heard thy prayer and thy supplication, that thou hast made before Me" (1 Kings 9:3). "Thy prayer is heard" (Luke 1:13). "Thus saith the Lord God of Israel, That which thou hast prayed to Me...I have heard" (2 Kings 19:20).

And there are still more promises. "He shall call upon Me, and I will answer him: I will be with Him in trouble; I will deliver him, and honour him" (Ps. 91:15). "Then shalt thou call, and the Lord shall answer; thou shalt cry, and He shall say, Here I am" (Isa. 58:9). "While they are yet speaking, I will hear" (Isa. 65:24). "They shall call on My name, and I will hear them: I will say, It is My people: and they shall say, The Lord is my God" (Zech. 13:9).

Pray alone, and, as you have opportunity, pray together: "They lifted up their voice to God with one accord" (Acts 4:24). "These all continued with one accord in prayer and supplication" (Acts 1:14). "Many were gathered together praying" (Acts 12:12). "We kneeled down on the shore and prayed" (Acts 21:5).

If ever earnest prayer was needed, it is now. Let your prayer be like that of Elijah, Jacob, and Christ: "He prayed earnestly" (James 5:17). "I will not [cannot] let Thee go, except thou bless me" (Gen. 32:26). "And being in an agony, He prayed more earnestly" (Luke 22:44)

The Wonderful Father will hear and help. May this little book encourage you daily toward that goal of unceasing, trustful prayer (Luke 18:1; Eph. 6:18; 1 Thess. 5:17). Yes, indeed, "ask, and ye shall receive, that your joy may be full" (John 16:24). As you do, remember the important qualifications found in 2 Chronicles 7:14, Jeremiah 29:13, Mark 11:24, James 5:16, and 1 John 3:22.

# Contents

# Chapter One

# *The Privilege of Prayer*

***Beholding the glory***—"The unveiled glory of God no man could look upon and live; but Moses is assured that he shall behold as much of the divine glory as he could bear in his present, mortal state. That Hand that made the world, that holds the mountains in their places, takes this man of dust—this man of mighty faith—and mercifully covers him in a cleft of the rock, while the glory of God and all His goodness pass before him. Can we marvel that 'the excellent glory' reflected from Omnipotence shone in Moses' face with such brightness that the people could not look upon it? The impress of God was upon him, making him appear as one of the shining angels from the throne.

"This experience, above all else the assurance that God would hear his prayer and that the divine presence would attend him, was of more value to Moses as a leader than the learning of Egypt or all his attainments in military science. No earthly power or skill or learning can supply the place of God's immediate presence. In the history of Moses we may see what intimate communion with God it is man's privilege to enjoy. To the transgressor it is a fearful thing to fall into the hands of the living God. But Moses was not afraid to be alone with the Author of that law which had been spoken with such grandeur from Mount Sinai, for his soul was in harmony with the will of his Maker.

"Prayer is the opening of the heart to God as to a friend. The eye of faith will discern God very near, and the suppliant may obtain precious evidence of the divine love and care for him…" (*Testimonies for the Church*, vol. 4, p. 533).

***The wonderful privilege***—"As yet the disciples were unacquainted with the Saviour's unlimited resources and power. He said to them, 'Hitherto have ye asked nothing in My name.' John 16:24. He explained that the secret of their success would be in asking for strength and grace in His name. He would be present before the Father to make request for them. The prayer of the humble suppliant He presents as His own desire in that soul's behalf. Every sincere prayer is heard in heaven. It may not be fluently expressed; but if the heart is in it, it will ascend to the sanctuary where Jesus ministers, and He will present it to the Father without one awkward, stammering word, beautiful and fragrant with the incense of His own perfection.

"The path of sincerity and integrity is not a path free from obstruction, but in every difficulty we are to see a call to prayer. There is no one living who has any power that he has not received from God, and the source whence it comes is open to

9

the weakest human being. 'Whatsoever ye shall ask in My name,' said Jesus, 'that will I do, that the Father may be glorified in the Son. If ye shall ask anything in My name, I will do it.'

" 'In My name,' Christ bade His disciples pray. In Christ's name His followers are to stand before God. Through the value of the sacrifice made for them, they are of value in the Lord's sight. Because of the imputed righteousness of Christ they are accounted precious. For Christ's sake the Lord pardons those that fear Him. He does not see in them the vileness of the sinner. He recognizes in them the likeness of His Son, in whom they believe" (*The Desire of Ages*, p. 667).

*No distrust of the future*—"The disciples no longer had any distrust of the future. They knew that Jesus was in heaven, and that His sympathies were with them still. They knew that they had a friend at the throne of God, and they were eager to present their requests to the Father in the name of Jesus. In solemn awe they bowed in prayer, repeating the assurance, 'Whatsoever ye shall ask the Father in My name, He will give it you. Hitherto have ye asked nothing in My name: ask, and ye shall receive, that your joy may be full.' John 16:23, 24. They extended the hand of faith higher and higher, with the mighty argument, 'It is Christ that died, yea rather, that is risen again, who is even at the right hand of God, who also maketh intercession for us.' Romans 8:34" (*The Desire of Ages*, p. 833).

*They do not realize* —"They do not realize what a great privilege and necessity are prayer, repentance, and the doing of the words of Christ" (*Selected Messages*, book 1, p. 134).

*Go to Jesus*—"There are few who rightly appreciate or improve the precious privilege of prayer. We should go to Jesus and tell Him all our needs. We may bring Him our little cares and perplexities as well as our greater troubles. Whatever arises to disturb or distress us, we should take it to the Lord in prayer. When we feel that we need the presence of Christ at every step, Satan will have little opportunity to intrude his temptations. It is his studied effort to keep us away from our best and most sympathizing friend. We should make no one our confidant but Jesus. We can safely commune with Him of all that is in our hearts" (*Testimonies for the Church*, vol. 5, pp. 200, 201).

*When at the Red Sea*—"When He brings His people into strait places, then it is their privilege to assemble together for prayer, remembering that all things come of God. Those who have not yet shared in the trying experiences that attend the work in these last days will soon have to pass through scenes that will severely test their confidence in God. It is at the time His people see no way to advance, when the Red

Sea is before them and the pursuing army behind, that God bids them: 'Go forward.' Thus He is working to test their faith. When such experiences come to you, go forward, trusting in Christ. Walk step by step in the path He marks out. Trials will come, but go forward. This will give you an experience that will strengthen your faith in God and fit you for truest service" (*Testimonies for the Church*, vol. 9, p. 273).

*A wonderful thing*—"It is a wonderful thing that we can pray effectually; that unworthy, erring mortals possess the power of offering their requests to God. What higher power can man desire than this—to be linked with the infinite God? Feeble, sinful man has the privilege of speaking to his Maker. We may utter words that reach the throne of the Monarch of the universe. We may speak with Jesus as we walk by the way, and He says, I am at thy right hand" (*Gospel Workers*, p. 258).

*We earnestly need it*—"Every day we need the discipline of self-humiliation, that we may be prepared to receive the heavenly gift, not to hoard it, not to rob God's children of His blessing, but to give it in all its rich fullness to others. When more than now shall we need a heart open to receive, aching, as it were, with its longing to impart?

"We are in duty bound to draw largely from the treasure house of divine knowledge. God wants us to receive much, in order that we may impart much. He desires us to be channels through which He can impart richly of His grace to the world.

"Let sincerity and faith characterize your prayers. The Lord is willing to do for us 'exceeding abundantly above all that we ask or think.' Ephesians 3:20. Talk it; pray it. Do not talk unbelief" (*Testimonies for the Church*, vol. 7, p. 273).

*In time of trial and temptaion*—"When in trouble, when assailed by fierce temptations, they have the privilege of prayer. What an exalted privilege! Finite beings, of dust and ashes, admitted through the mediation of Christ, into the audience chamber of the Most High. In such exercises the soul is brought into a sacred nearness with God and is renewed in knowledge and true holiness and fortified against the assaults of the enemy" (*Child Guidance*, p. 468).

*Entering upon the privilege*—"Rest yourself wholly in the hands of Jesus. Contemplate His great love, and while you meditate upon His self-denial, His infinite sacrifice made in our behalf in order that we should believe in Him, your heart will be filled with holy joy, calm peace, and indescribable love. As we talk of Jesus, as we call upon Him in prayer, our confidence that He is our personal, loving Saviour will strengthen, and His character will appear more and more lovely.... We may enjoy rich feasts of love, and as we fully believe that we are His by adoption, we may have a foretaste of heaven. Wait upon the Lord in faith. The Lord draws out the soul in prayer, and gives us to feel His precious love. We have a nearness to Him, and can hold sweet communion with Him. We obtain distinct views of His tenderness and compassion, and our hearts are broken and melted with contemplation of the love that is given to us. We feel indeed an abiding Christ in the soul....Our peace is like a river, wave after wave of glory rolls into the heart, and indeed we sup with Jesus and He with us. We have a realizing sense of the love of God, and we rest in His love. No language can describe it, it is beyond knowledge. We are one with Christ, our life is hid with Christ in God. We have the assurance that when He who is our life shall appear, then shall we also appear with Him in glory. With strong confidence, we can call God our Father. Whether we live or die, we are the Lord's. His Spirit makes us like Jesus Christ in temper, and disposition, and we represent Christ to others. When Christ is abiding in the soul the fact cannot be hid; for He is like a well of water springing up into everlasting life. We can but represent the likeness of Christ in our character, and our words, our deportment, produces in others a deep, abiding, increasing love for Jesus, and we make manifest...that we are conformed to the image of Jesus Christ" (*Sons and Daughters of God*, p. 311).

*- Chapter Two -*

# Genuine, Heartfelt Prayer

***A conversation with God***—"If we keep the Lord ever before us, allowing our hearts to go out in thanksgiving and praise to Him, we shall have a continual freshness in our religious life. Our prayers will take the form of a conversation with God as we would talk with a friend. He will speak His mysteries to us personally. Often there will come to us a sweet joyful sense of the presence of Jesus. Often our hearts will burn within us as He draws nigh to commune with us as He did with Enoch. When this is in truth the experience of the Christian, there is, seen in his life a simplicity, a humility, meekness, and lowliness of heart, that shows to all with whom he associates that he has been with Jesus and learned of Him" (*Christ's Object Lessons*, pp. 129, 130).

***Opening the heart to God***—"Prayer is the opening of the heart to God as to a friend. Not that it is necessary in order to make known to God what we are, but in order to enable us to receive Him. Prayer does not bring God down to us, but brings us up to Him" (*Steps to Christ*, p. 93).

***The hand of faith holds the key***—"The darkness of the evil one encloses those who neglect to pray. The whispered temptations of the enemy entice them to sin; and it is all because they do not make use of the privileges that God has given them in the divine appointment of prayer. Why should the sons and daughters of God be reluctant to pray, when prayer is the key in the hand of faith to unlock heaven's storehouse, where are treasured the boundless resources of Omnipotence? Without unceasing prayer and diligent watching we are in danger of growing careless and of deviating from the right path" (*Steps to Christ*, pp. 94, 95).

*The very soul of religion*—"Do not neglect prayer, for it is the soul of religion. With earnest, fervent prayer, plead for purity of soul. Plead as earnestly, as eagerly, as you would for your mortal life, were it at stake. Remain before God until unutterable longings are begotten within you for salvation, and the sweet evidence is obtained of pardoned sin" (*Testimonies for the Church*, vol. 1, p. 163).

*The secret of spiritual power*—"Prayer is the breath of the soul. It is the secret of spiritual power. No other means of grace can be substituted, and the health of the soul be preserved. Prayer brings the heart into immediate contact with the Wellspring of life, and strengthens the sinew and muscle of the religious experience. Neglect the exercise of prayer, or engage in prayer spasmodically, now and then, as seems convenient, and you lose your hold on God" (*Gospel Workers,* pp. 254, 255).

- Chapter Three -

# Daily Prayer a Necessity

*As essential as food*—"Daily prayer is as essential to growth in grace, and even to spiritual life itself, as is temporal food to physical well-being. We should accustom ourselves to often lift the thoughts to God in prayer. If the mind wanders, we must bring it back; by persevering effort, habit will finally make it easy. We cannot for one moment separate ourselves from Christ with safety. We may have His presence to attend us at every step, but only by observing the conditions which He has Himself laid down" (*Messages to Young People*, p. 115).

*The needed preparation*—"Several times each day precious, golden moments should be consecrated to prayer and the study of the Scriptures, if it is only to commit a text to memory, that spiritual life may exist in the soul. The varied interests of the cause furnish us with food for reflection and inspiration for our prayers. Communion with God is highly essential for spiritual health, and here only may be obtained that wisdom and correct judgment so necessary in the performance of every duty.

"The strength acquired in prayer to God, united with individual effort in training the mind to thoughtfulness and care-taking, prepares the person for daily duties and keeps the spirit in peace under all circumstances, however trying. The temptations to which we are daily exposed make prayer a necessity. In order that we may be kept by the power of God through faith, the desires of the mind should be continually ascending in silent prayer for help, for light, for strength, for knowledge. But thought and prayer cannot take the place of earnest, faithful improvement of time. Work and prayer are both required in perfecting Christian character.

"We must live a twofold life—a life of thought and action, of silent prayer and earnest work. All who have received the light of truth should feel it their duty to shed rays of light upon the pathway of the impenitent. We should be witnesses for Christ in our offices as verily as in the church. God requires us to be living epistles, known and read of all men. The soul that turns to God for its strength, its support, its power, by daily, earnest prayer, will have noble aspirations, clear perceptions of truth and duty, lofty purposes of action, and a continual hungering and thirsting after righteousness. By maintaining a connection with God we shall be enabled to diffuse to others, through our association with them, the light, the peace, the serenity, that rules in our hearts, and set before them an example of unwavering fidelity to the interests of the work in which we are engaged" (*Testimonies for the Church,* vol. 4, pp. 459, 460).

***Combining prayer with labor***—"The spirit of unselfish labor for others gives depth, stability, and Christlike loveliness to the character and brings peace and happiness to its possessor. The aspirations are elevated. There is no room for sloth or selfishness. Those who exercise the Christian graces will grow. They will have spiritual sinew and muscle, and will be strong to work for God. They will have clear spiritual perceptions, a steady, increasing faith, and prevailing power in prayer" (*Testimonies for the Church*, vol. 5, p. 607).

***Connecting with heaven***—"Those who will put on the whole armor of God and devote some time every day to meditation and prayer and to the study of the Scriptures will be connected with heaven and will have a saving, transforming influence upon those around them. Great thoughts, noble aspirations, clear perceptions of truth and duty to God, will be theirs. They will be yearning for purity, for light, for love, for all the graces of heavenly birth. Their earnest prayers will enter into that within the veil. This class will have a sanctified boldness to come into the presence of the Infinite One. They will feel that heaven's light and glories are for them, and they will become refined, elevated, ennobled by this intimate acquaintance with God. Such is the privilege of true Christians.

"Abstract meditation is not enough; busy action is not enough; both are essential to the formation of Christian character. Strength acquired in earnest, secret prayer prepares us to withstand the allurements of society. And yet we should not exclude ourselves from the world, for our Christian experience is to be the light of the world. The society of unbelievers will do us no harm if we mingle with them for the purpose of connecting them with God and are strong enough spiritually to withstand their influence.

"Christ came into the world to save it, to connect fallen man with the infinite God. Christ's followers are to be channels of light. Maintaining communion with God, they are to transmit to those in darkness and error the choice blessings which they receive of heaven. Enoch did not become polluted with the iniquities existing in his day; why need we in our day?" (*Testimonies for the Church*, vol. 5, pp. 112, 113).

*Needed by our youth*—"The trials and privations of which so many youth complain, Christ endured without murmuring. And this discipline is the very experience the youth need, which will give firmness to their characters, and make them like Christ, strong in spirit to resist temptation. They will not, if they separate from the influence of those who would lead them astray and corrupt their morals, be overcome by the devices of Satan. Through daily prayer to God, they will have wisdom and grace from Him to bear the conflict and stern realities of life, and come off victorious. Fidelity and serenity of mind can only be retained by watchfulness and prayer" (*Messages to Young People*, p. 80).

*The core of religion*—"Religion must begin with emptying and purifying the heart, and must be nurtured by daily prayer" (*Testimonies for the Church*, vol. 4, p. 535).

*Wherever you are sent*—"Wherever you may be sent, cherish in your hearts and minds the fear and love of God. Go daily to the Lord for instruction and guidance; depend upon God for light and knowledge. Pray for this instruction and this light, until you get it. It will not avail for you to ask, and then forget the thing for which you prayed. Keep your mind upon your prayer. You can do this while working with your hands. You can say, Lord, I believe; with all my heart I believe. Let the Holy Spirit's power come upon me.

"If there were more praying among us, more, exercise of a living faith, and less dependence upon some one else to have an experience for us, we would be far in advance of where we are to-day in spiritual intelligence. What we need is a deep, individual heart and soul experience. Then we shall be able to tell what God is doing and how He is working. We need to have a living experience in the things of God; and we are not safe unless we have this. There are some who have a good experience, and they tell you about it; but when you come to weigh it up, you see that it is not a correct experience, for it is not in accordance with a plain, Thus saith the Lord. If ever there was a time in our history when we needed to humble our individual souls before God, it is to-day. We need to come to God with faith in all that is promised in the word, and then walk in all the light and power that God gives" (*Fundamentals of Christian Education*, pp. 530, 531).

**Whatever you do**—"We are to look upon every duty, however humble, as sacred because it is a part of God's service. Our daily prayer should be, 'Lord, help me to do my best. Teach me how to do better work. Give me energy and cheerfulness. Help me to bring into my service the loving ministry of the Saviour' " (*The Ministry of Healing*, p. 474).

*- Chapter Four -*

# The Morning Prayer

**Enter the day with prayer**—"Let your day be entered upon with prayer; work as in God's sight" (*Testimonies for the Church*, vol. 4, p. 588).

**Begin the day by your bedside**—"It is our privilege to open our hearts, and let the sunshine of Christ's presence in. My brother, my sister, face the light. Come into actual personal contact with Christ, that you may exert an influence that is uplifting and reviving. Let your faith be strong and pure and steadfast. Let gratitude to God fill your hearts. When you rise in the morning, kneel at your bedside, and ask God to give you strength to fulfill the duties of the day, and to meet its temptations. Ask Him to help you to bring into your work Christ's sweetness of character. Ask Him to help you to speak words that will inspire those around you with hope and courage, and draw you nearer to the Saviour" (*Sons and Daughters of God*, p. 199).

**The first word upon arising**—"The very first outbreathing of the soul in the morning should be for the presence of Jesus. 'Without Me,' He says, 'ye can do nothing.' It is Jesus that we need; His light, His life, His spirit, must be ours continually. We need Him every hour. And we should pray in the morning that as the sun illuminates the landscape, and fills the world with light, so the Sun of Righteousness may shine into the chambers of mind and heart, and make us all light in the Lord. We cannot do without His presence one moment. The enemy knows when we undertake to do without our Lord, and he is there, ready to fill our minds with his evil suggestions that we may fall from our steadfastness; but it is the desire of the Lord that from moment to moment we should abide in Him, and thus be complete in Him" (*My Life Today*, p. 15).

***Your very first work***—"Consecrate yourself to God in the morning; make this your very first work. Let your prayer be, 'Take me, O Lord, as wholly Thine. I lay all my plans at Thy feet. Use me today in Thy service. Abide in me, and let all my work be wrought in Thee.' This is a daily matter. Each morning consecrate yourself to God for that day. Surrender all your plans to Him, to be carried out or given up as His providence shall indicate. Thus day by day you may be giving your life into the hands of God, and thus your life will be molded more and more after the life of Christ. A life in Christ is a life of restfulness. There may be no ecstasy of feeling, but there should be an abiding, peaceful trust" (*Steps to Christ,* p. 70).

***Our daily prayer***—"In the future life the mysteries that here have annoyed and disappointed us will be made plain. We shall see that our seemingly unanswered prayers and disappointed hopes have been among our greatest blessings. We are to look upon every duty, however humble, as sacred because it is a part of God's service. Our daily prayer should be, 'Lord, help me to do my best. Teach me how to do better work. Give me energy and cheerfulness. Help me to bring into my service the loving ministry of the Saviour'" (*The Ministry of Healing,* p. 474).

***The first lesson***—"The first lesson to be taught the workers in our institutions is the lesson of dependence upon God. Before they can attain success in any line, they must, each for himself, accept the truth contained in the words of Christ: 'Without Me ye can do nothing.'

"Righteousness has its root in godliness. No human being is righteous any longer than he has faith in God and maintains a vital connection with Him. As a flower of the field has its root in the soil; as it must receive air, dew, showers, and sunshine, so must we receive from God that which ministers to the life of the soul. It is only through becoming partakers of His nature that we receive power to obey His commandments. No man, high or low, experienced or inexperienced, can steadily maintain before his fellowmen a pure, forceful life unless his life is hid with Christ in God. The greater the activity among men, the closer should be the communion of the heart with God....

"Every morning take time to begin your work with prayer. Do not think this wasted time; it is time that will live through eternal ages. By this means success and spiritual victory will be brought in. The machinery will respond to the touch of the Master's hand. God's blessing is certainly worth asking for, and the work cannot be done aright unless the beginning is right" (*Testimonies for the Church,* vol. 7, p. 194).

***When you rise***—"When you rise in the morning, do you feel your helplessness and your need of strength from God? and do you humbly, heartily make known your wants to your heavenly Father? If so, angels mark your prayers, and if these prayers have not gone forth out of feigned lips, when you are in danger of unconsciously doing wrong and exerting an influence which will lead others to do wrong, your guardian angel will be by your side, prompting you to a better course, choosing your words for you, and influencing your actions.

"If you feel in no danger, and if you offer no prayer for help and strength to resist temptations, you will be sure to go astray; your neglect of duty will be marked in the book of God in heaven, and you will be found wanting in the trying day" (*Testimonies for the Church*, vol. 3, pp. 363, 364).

- *Chapter Five* -

# *Fervent Prayer*

***Keep asking***—"God does not say, Ask once, and you shall receive. He bids us ask. Unwearyingly persist in prayer. The persistent asking brings the petitioner into a more earnest attitude, and gives him an increased desire to receive the things for which he asks.

"But many have not a living faith. This is why they do not see more of the power of God....They plan and devise, but pray little, and have little real trust in God. They think they have faith, but it is only the impulse of the moment. Failing to realize their own need, or God's willingness to give, they do not persevere in keeping their requests before the Lord.

"Our prayers are to be as earnest and persistent as was the petition of the needy friend who asked for the loaves at midnight. The more earnestly and steadfastly we ask, the closer will be our spiritual union with Christ" (*Christ's Object Lessons*, pp. 145, 146).

***Fervent, constant prayer***—"If the Saviour of men, the Son of God, felt the need of prayer, how much more should feeble, sinful mortals feel the necessity of fervent, constant prayer.

"Our heavenly Father waits to bestow upon us the fullness of His blessing. It is our privilege to drink largely at the fountain of boundless love. What a wonder it is that we pray so little! God is ready and willing to hear the sincere prayer of the humblest of His children....

"Why should the sons and daughters of God be reluctant to pray, when prayer is the key in the hand of faith to unlock heaven's storehouse, where are treasured the boundless resources of Omnipotence?" (*Steps to Christ*, pp. 94, 95).

*The prayer of faith*—"Faith is not feeling....True faith is in no sense allied to presumption. Only he who has true faith is secure against presumption, for presumption is Satan's counterfeit of faith....

"To talk of religion in a casual way, to pray without soul-hunger and living faith, avails nothing....

"Many hold faith as an opinion. But saving faith is a transaction, by which those who receive Christ join themselves in covenant relation with God. Genuine faith is life. A living faith means an increase of vigor, a confiding trust, by which the soul becomes a conquering power" (*Gospel Workers,* pp. 260, 261).

- Chapter Six -

# The Prayer of Faith

*Bearing the prayer of faith to heaven*—"They [the angels] hear the offering of praise and the prayer of faith, and they bear the petitions to Him who ministers in the sanctuary for His people and offers His merits in their behalf" (*Counsels to Parents, Teachers, and Students,* p. 110).

*Praying in faith*—"There are many who, though striving to obey God's commandments, have little peace or joy. This lack in their experience is the result of a failure to exercise faith. They walk as it were in a salt land, a parched wilderness. They claim little, when they might claim much; for there is no limit to the promises of God. Such ones do not correctly represent the sanctification that comes through obedience to the truth. The Lord would have all His sons and daughters happy, peaceful, and obedient. Through the exercise of faith the believer comes into possession of these blessings. Through faith, every deficiency of character may be supplied, every defilement cleansed, every fault corrected, every excellence developed.

"Prayer is heaven's ordained means of success in the conflict with sin and the development of Christian character. The divine influences that come in answer to the prayer of faith will accomplish in the soul of the suppliant all for which he pleads. For the pardon of sin, for the Holy Spirit, for a Christlike temper, for wisdom and strength to do His work, for any gift He promised, we may ask; and the promise is, 'Ye shall receive' " (*The Acts of the Apostles,* pp. 563, 564).

*Moving the arm*—"By your fervent prayers of faith you can move the arm that moves the world" (*The Adventist Home,* p. 264).

***Part of God's plan***—"Worldly wisdom teaches that prayer is not essential. Men of science claim that there can be no real answer to prayer; that this would be a violation of law, a miracle, and that miracles have no existence. The universe, say they, is governed by fixed laws, and God Himself does nothing contrary to these laws. Thus they represent God as bound by His own laws as if the operation of divine laws could exclude divine freedom. Such teaching is opposed to the testimony of the Scriptures. Were not miracles wrought by Christ and His apostles? The same compassionate Saviour lives today, and He is as willing to listen to the prayer of faith as when He walked visibly among men. The natural co-operates with the supernatural. It is part of God's plan to grant us, in answer to the prayer of faith, that which He would not bestow did we not thus ask" (*The Great Controversy,* p. 525).

***What is the prayer of faith?***—"Prayer is not an expiation for sin; it has no virtue or merit of itself. All the flowery words at our command are not equivalent to one holy desire. The most eloquent prayers are but idle words if they do not express the true sentiments of the heart. But the prayer that comes from an earnest heart, when the simple wants of the soul are expressed, as we would ask an earthly friend for a favor, expecting it to be granted this is the prayer of faith. God does not desire our ceremonial compliments, but the unspoken cry of the heart broken and subdued with a sense of its sin and utter weakness finds its way to the Father of all mercy" (*Thoughts from the Mount of Blessing,* pp. 86, 87).

***When Satan trembles***—"If Satan sees that he is in danger of losing one soul, he will exert himself to the utmost to keep that one. And when the individual is aroused to his danger, and, with distress and fervor, looks to Jesus for strength, Satan fears that he will lose a captive, and he calls a reinforcement of his angels to hedge in the poor soul, and form a wall of darkness around him, that heaven's light may not reach him. But if the one in danger perseveres, and in his helplessness casts himself upon the merits of the blood of Christ, our Saviour listens to the earnest prayer of faith, and sends a reinforcement of those angels that excel in strength to deliver him. Satan cannot endure to have his powerful rival appealed to, for he fears and trembles before His strength and majesty. At the sound of fervent prayer, Satan's whole host trembles. He continues to call legions of evil angels to accomplish his object. And when angels, all-powerful, clothed with the armory of heaven, come to the help of the fainting, pursued soul, Satan and his host fall back, well knowing that their battle is lost. The willing subjects of Satan are faithful, active, and united in one object. And although they hate and war with one another, yet they improve every opportunity to advance their common interest. But the great Commander in heaven and earth has limited Satan's power" (*Testimonies to the Church,* vol. 1, p. 346).

***Baffling Satan***—"Man is Satan's captive and is naturally inclined to follow his suggestions and do his bidding. He has in himself no power to oppose effectual resistance to evil. It is only as Christ abides in him by living faith, influencing his desires and strengthening him with strength from above, that man may venture to face so terrible a foe. Every other means of defense is utterly vain. It is only through Christ that Satan's power is limited. This is a momentous truth that all should understand. Satan is busy every moment, going to and fro, walking up and down in the earth, seeking whom he may devour. But the earnest prayer of faith will baffle his strongest efforts. Then take 'the shield of faith,' brethren, 'wherewith ye shall be able to quench the fiery darts of the wicked' " (*Testimonies for the Church,* vol. 5, p. 294).

***The great strength of the Christian***—"The prayer of faith is the great strength of the Christian and will assuredly prevail against Satan. This is why he insinuates that we have no need of prayer. The name of Jesus, our Advocate, he detests; and when we earnestly come to Him for help, Satan's host is alarmed. It serves his purpose well if we neglect the exercise of prayer, for then his lying wonders are more readily received" (*Testimonies for the Church,* vol. 1, p. 296).

***It is never lost***—"The prayer of faith is never lost; but to claim that it will be always answered in the very way and for the particular thing we have expected, is presumption" (*Testimonies for the Church,* vol. 1, p. 231).

***Fix your eyes upon Him***—"My dear fellow workers, be true, hopeful, heroic. Let every blow be made in faith. As you do your best, the Lord will reward your faithfulness. From the life-giving fountain draw physical, mental, and spiritual energy. Manliness, womanliness sanctified, purified, refined, ennobled we have the promise of receiving. We need that faith which will enable us to endure the seeing of Him who is invisible. As you fix your eyes upon Him, you will be filled with a deep love for the souls for whom He died, and will receive strength for renewed effort.

"Christ is our only hope. Come to God in the name of Him who gave His life for the world. Rely upon the efficacy of His sacrifice. Show that His love, His joy, is in your soul, and that because of this your joy is full. Cease to talk unbelief. In God is our strength. Pray much. Prayer is the life of the soul. The prayer of faith is the weapon by which we may successfully resist every assault of the enemy" (*Selected Messages,* book 1, p. 88).

***The Spirit sent in answer to***—"At all times and in all places, in all sorrows and in all afflictions, when the outlook seems dark and the future perplexing, and we feel helpless and alone, the Comforter will be sent in answer to the prayer of faith. Circumstances may separate us from every earthly friend; but no circumstance, no distance, can separate us from the heavenly Comforter. Wherever we are, wherever we may go, He is always at our right hand to support, sustain, uphold, and cheer" (*The Desire of Ages,* pp. 669, 670).

**Help will come**—"Power will come from God to man in answer to the prayer of faith" (*Testimonies for the Church,* vol. 4, p. 402).

*- Chapter Seven -*

# The Science of Prayer

**This is the science of prayer**—" 'Commit thy way unto the Lord; trust also in Him; and He shall bring it to pass....He will bring forth thy righteousness as the light, and thy judgment as the noonday.' Psalm 35:5, 6.

" 'The Lord also will be a refuge for the oppressed, a refuge in times of trouble. And they that know Thy name will put their trust in Thee: for Thou, Lord, hast not forsaken them that seek Thee.' Psalm 9:9, 10.

"The compassion that God manifests toward us, He bids us manifest toward others. Let the impulsive, the self-sufficient, the revengeful, behold the meek and lowly One, led as a lamb to the slaughter, unretaliating as a sheep dumb before her shearers. Let them look upon Him whom our sins have pierced and our sorrows burdened, and they will learn to endure, to forbear, and to forgive.

"Through faith in Christ, every deficiency of character may be supplied, every defilement cleansed, every fault corrected, every excellence developed.

" 'Ye are complete in Him.' Colossians 2:10.

"Prayer and faith are closely allied, and they need to be studied together. In the prayer of faith there is a divine science; it is a science that everyone who would make his lifework a success must understand. Christ says, 'What things soever ye desire, when ye pray, believe that ye receive them, and ye shall have them.' Mark 11:24. He makes it plain that our asking must be according to God's will; we must ask for the things that He has promised, and whatever we receive must be used in doing His will. The conditions met, the promise is unequivocal.

"For the pardon of sin, for the Holy Spirit, for a Christlike temper, for wisdom and strength to do His work, for any gift He has promised, we may ask; then we are to believe that we receive, and return thanks to God that we have received.

"We need look for no outward evidence of the blessing. The gift is in the promise, and we may go about our work assured that what God has promised He is able to perform, and that the gift, which we already possess, will be realized when we need it most.

"To live thus by the word of God means the surrender to Him of the whole life. There will be felt a continual sense of need and dependence, a drawing out of the heart after God. Prayer is a necessity; for it is the life of the soul. Family prayer, public prayer, have their place; but it is secret communion with God that sustains the soul life.

"It was in the mount with God that Moses beheld the pattern of that wonderful building which was to be the abiding place of His glory. It is in the mount with God in the secret place of communion that we are to contemplate His glorious ideal for humanity. Thus we shall be enabled so to fashion our character building that to us may be fulfilled His promise, 'I will dwell in them, and walk in them; and I will be their God, and they shall be My people.' 2 Corinthians 6:16.

"It was in hours of solitary prayer that Jesus in His earthly life received wisdom and power. Let the youth follow His example in finding at dawn and twilight a quiet season for communion with their Father in heaven. And throughout the day let them lift up their hearts to God. At every step of our way He says, 'I the Lord thy God will hold thy right hand,… Fear not; I will help thee." Isaiah 41:13. Could our children learn these lessons in the morning of their years, what freshness and power, what joy and sweetness, would be brought into their lives!" (*Education,* pp. 257-259).

*More on this divine science*—"Christ's lessons in regard to prayer should be carefully considered. There is a divine science in prayer, and His illustration brings to view principles that all need to understand. He shows what is the true spirit of prayer, He teaches the necessity of perseverance in presenting our requests to God, and assures us of His willingness to hear and answer prayer" (*Christ's Object Lessons,* p. 142).

(Read the chapter "Asking to Give" in *Christ's Object Lessons,* pp. 139-149, for many more principles regarding the science of prayer.)

- Chapter Eight -

# When Much Prayer is Needed

*For progress in the divine life*—"Heaven is not closed against the fervent prayers of the righteous. Elijah was a man subject to like passions as we are, yet the Lord heard and in a most striking manner answered his petitions. The only reason for our lack of power with God is to be found in ourselves. If the inner life of many who profess the truth were presented before them, they would not claim to be Christians. They are not growing in grace. A hurried prayer is offered now and then, but there is no real communion with God.

"We must be much in prayer if we would make progress in the divine life. When the message of truth was first proclaimed, how much we prayed. How often was the voice of intercession heard in the chamber, in the barn, in the orchard, or the grove. Frequently we spent hours in earnest prayer, two or three together claiming the promise; often the sound of weeping was heard and then the voice of thanksgiving and the song of praise. Now the day of God is nearer than when we first believed, and we should be more earnest, more zealous, and fervent than in those early days. Our perils are greater now than then. Souls are more hardened. We need now to be imbued with the spirit of Christ, and we should not rest until we receive it" (*Testimonies for the Church,* vol. 5, pp. 161, 162).

*For higher Christian attainments*—"Paul knew that the higher Christian attainments can be reached only through much prayer and constant watchfulness, and this he tried to instill into their minds. But he knew also that in Christ crucified they were offered power sufficient to convert the soul and divinely adapted to enable them to resist all temptations to evil. With faith in God as their armor, and with His word as their weapon of warfare, they would be supplied with an inner power that would enable them to turn aside the attacks of the enemy" (*The Acts of the Apostles,* p. 307).

*In the study of the Bible*—"Read your Bible with much prayer. Do not try to humble others, but humble yourselves before God, and deal gently with one another" (*Selected Messages,* book 2, p. 328).

*Preparation for the work that needs to be done*—"Moses would never have been prepared for his position of trust had he waited for God to do the work for him. Light from heaven will come to those who feel the need of it, and who seek for it as for hidden treasures. But if we sink down into a state of inactivity, willing to be controlled by Satan's power, God will not send His inspiration to us. Unless we exert to the utmost the powers which He has given us, we shall ever remain weak and inefficient. Much prayer and the most vigorous exercise of the mind are necessary if we would be prepared to do the work which God would entrust to us. Many never attain to the position which they might occupy, because they wait for God to do for them that which He has given them power to do for themselves. All who are fitted for usefulness in this life must be trained by the severest mental and moral discipline, and then God will assist them by combining divine power with human effort" (*Testimonies for the Church,* vol. 4, p. 611).

*Carrying on the work of God*—"As activity increases and men become successful in doing any work for God, there is danger of trusting to human plans and methods. There is a tendency to pray less, and to have less faith. Like the disciples, we are in danger of losing sight of our dependence on God, and seeking to make a savior of our activity. We need to look constantly to Jesus, realizing that it is His power which does the work. While we are to labor earnestly for the salvation of the lost, we must also take time for meditation, for prayer, and for the study of the word of God. Only the work accomplished with much prayer, and sanctified by the merit of Christ, will in the end prove to have been efficient for good" (*The Desire of Ages,* p. 362).

***Doing pioneer work in new areas***—"In new fields, much prayer and wise labor are needed. There are wanted, not merely men who can sermonize, but those who have an experimental knowledge of the mystery of godliness, and who can meet the urgent needs of the people those who realize the importance of their position as servants of Jesus, and will cheerfully take up the cross that He has taught them how to bear" (*Gospel Workers,* p. 191).

***Reaching hearts***—"Through much prayer you must labor for souls, for this is the only method by which you can reach hearts. It is not your work, but the work of Christ who is by your side, that impresses hearts" (*Evangelism,* p. 342).

***For a better home***—"Affections cannot be lasting, even in the home circle, unless there is a conformity of the will and disposition to the will of God. All the faculties and passions are to be brought into harmony with the attributes of Jesus Christ. If the father and mother in the love and fear of God unite their interests to have authority in the home, they will see the necessity of much prayer, much sober reflection. And as they seek God, their eyes will be opened to see heavenly messengers present to protect them in answer to the prayer of faith. They will overcome the weaknesses of their character and go on unto perfection" (*The Adventist Home,* pp. 315, 316).

***Separating truth from error***—"Satan's angels are wise to do evil, and they will create that which some will claim to be advanced light, and will proclaim it as new and wonderful; yet while in some respects the message may be truth, it will be mingled with human inventions, and will teach for doctrine the commandments of men. If there was ever a time when we should watch and pray in real earnest, it is now. Many apparently good things will need to be carefully considered with much prayer, for they are specious devices of the enemy to lead souls in a path which lies so close to the path of truth that it will be scarcely distinguishable from it. But the eye of faith may discern that it is diverging, though almost imperceptibly, from the right path. At first it may be thought positively right, but after a while it is seen to be widely divergent from the way which leads to holiness and heaven" (*Evangelism,* p. 590).

***Seeking the Holy Spirit***—"We should daily receive the holy oil, that we may impart to others. All may be light bearers to the world if they will. We are to sink self out of sight in Jesus. We are to receive the word of the Lord in counsel and instruction, and gladly communicate it. There is now need of much prayer. Christ commands, 'Pray without ceasing;' that is, keep the mind uplifted to God, the source of all power and efficiency" (*Testimonies to Ministers and Gospel Workers,* p. 511).

***Standing on the unpopular side***—"It takes moral courage, firmness, decision, perseverance, and very much prayer to step out on the unpopular side. We are thankful that we can come to Christ as the poor suffering ones came to Christ in the temple" (*Evangelism,* p. 240).

***For victory over sin***—"God alone can give us the victory. He desires us to have the mastery over ourselves, our own will and ways. But He cannot work in us without our consent and co-operation. The divine Spirit works through the faculties and powers given to man. Our energies are required to co-operate with God.

"The victory is not won without much earnest prayer, without the humbling of self at every step. Our will is not to be forced into co-operation with divine agencies, but it must be voluntarily submitted" (*Thoughts from the Mount of Blessing,* p. 142).

***To wake up***—"Satanic agencies in human form will take part in this last great conflict to oppose the building up of the kingdom of God. And heavenly angels in human guise will be on the field of action. Men and women have confederated to oppose the Lord God of heaven, and the church is only half awake to the situation. There needs to be much more of prayer, much more of earnest effort among professed believers" (*S.D.A. Bible Commentary*, vol. 4, p. 1142; Letter 42, 1909).

# Chapter Nine

# *Praying for a Spiritual Revival*

***A revival of true Godliness***—"A revival of true godliness among us is the greatest and most urgent of all our needs. To seek this should be our first work. There must be earnest effort to obtain the blessing of the Lord, not because God is not willing to bestow His blessing upon us, but because we are unprepared to receive it. Our heavenly Father is more willing to give His Holy Spirit to them that ask Him, than are earthly parents to give good gifts to their children. But it is our work, by confession, humiliation, repentance, and earnest prayer, to fulfill the conditions upon which God has promised to grant us His blessing. A revival need be expected only in answer to prayer" (*Selected Messages,* book 1, p. 121).

***Removing the hindrances***—"There is nothing that Satan fears so much as that the people of God shall clear the way by removing every hindrance, so that the Lord can pour out His Spirit upon a languishing church and an impenitent congregation. If Satan had his way, there would never be another awakening, great or small, to the end of time. But we are not ignorant of his devices. It is possible to resist his power. When the way is prepared for the Spirit of God, the blessings will come. Satan can no more hinder a shower of blessing from descending upon God's people than he can close the windows of heaven that rain cannot come upon the earth. Wicked men and devils cannot hinder the work of God, or shut out His presence from the assemblies of His people, if they will, with subdued, contrite hearts, confess and put away their sins, and in faith claim His promises" (*Selected Messages,* book 1, p. 124).

***In answer to prayer***—"Only to those who wait humbly upon God, who watch for His guidance and grace, is the Spirit given. The power of God awaits their demand and reception. This promised blessing, claimed by faith, brings all other blessings in its train" (*The Desire of Ages,* p. 672).

***The outpouring***—"The Spirit came upon the waiting, praying disciples with a fullness that reached every heart. The Infinite One revealed Himself in power to His church. It was as if for ages this influence had been held in restraint, and now Heaven rejoiced in being able to pour out upon the church the riches of the Spirit's grace. And under the influence of the Spirit, words of penitence and confession mingled with songs of praise for sins forgiven. Words of thanksgiving and of prophecy were heard. All heaven bent low to behold and to adore the wisdom of matchless, incomprehensible love.... And what followed? The sword of the Spirit, newly edged

- Power of Prayer

with power and bathed in the lightnings of heaven, cut its way through unbelief. Thousands were converted in a day" (*The Acts of the Apostles,* p. 38).

- Chapter Ten -

# The Power in Prayer

*Not valued as it shoul be*—"We, too, must have times set apart for meditation and prayer and for receiving spiritual refreshing. We do not value the power and efficacy of prayer as we should. Prayer and faith will do what no power on earth can accomplish. We are seldom, in all respects, placed in the same position twice. We continually have new scenes and new trials to pass through, where past experience cannot be a sufficient guide. We must have the continual light that comes from God" (*The Ministry of Healing,* p. 509).

*Aided by thanksgiving and praise*—"Shall all our devotional exercises consist in asking and receiving? Shall we be always thinking of our wants and never of the benefits we receive? Shall we be recipients of His mercies and never express our gratitude to God, never praise Him for what He has done for us? We do not pray any too much, but we are too sparing of giving thanks. If the loving-kindness of God called forth more thanksgiving and praise, we would have far more power in prayer. We would abound more and more in the love of God and have more bestowed to praise Him for. You who complain that God does not hear your prayers, change your present order and mingle praise with your petitions. When you consider His goodness and mercies you will find that He will consider your wants.

"Pray, pray earnestly and without ceasing, but do not forget to praise. It becomes every child of God to vindicate His character. You can magnify the Lord; you can show the power of sustaining grace" (*Testimonies for the Church,* vol. 5, p. 317).

*A power for good*—"[Public] prayer, if properly offered, is a power for good. It is one of the means used by the Lord to communicate to the people the precious treasures of truth. But prayer is not what it should be, because of the defective voices of those who utter it" (*Testimonies for the Church,* vol. 6, p. 382).

*Keep going to the mercy seat*—"Without unceasing prayer and diligent watching we are in danger of growing careless and of deviating from the right path. The adversary seeks continually to obstruct the way to the mercy seat, that we may not by earnest supplication and faith obtain grace and power to resist temptation" (*Steps to Christ,* p. 95).

***Wins the power to our aid***— " 'I prayed,' he said, 'to the God of heaven.' In that brief prayer Nehemiah pressed into the presence of the King of kings and won to his side a power that can turn hearts as the rivers of waters are turned.

"To pray as Nehemiah prayed in his hour of need is a resource at the command of the Christian under circumstances when other forms of prayer may be impossible" (*Prophets and Kings,* p. 631).

***Needed by colporteurs***—"Those in the darkness of error are the purchase of the blood of Christ. They are the fruit of His suffering, and they are to be labored for. Let our canvassers know that it is for the advancement of Christ's kingdom that they are laboring. He will teach them as they go forth to their God-appointed work, to warn the world of a soon-coming judgment. Accompanied by the power of persuasion, the power of prayer, the power of the love of God, the evangelist's work will not, cannot, be without fruit" (*Colporteur Ministry*, p. 108).

***That power is real power***—"The glory that rested upon Christ is a pledge of the love of God for us. It tells us of the power of prayer, how the human voice may reach the ear of God, and our petitions find acceptance in the courts of heaven. By sin, earth was cut off from heaven, and alienated from its communion; but Jesus has connected it again with the sphere of glory. His love has encircled man, and reached the highest heaven. The light which fell from the open portals upon the head of our Saviour will fall upon us as we pray for help to resist temptation. The voice which spoke to Jesus says to every believing soul, This is My beloved child, in whom I am well pleased" (*The Desire of Ages,* p. 113).

***The heart of the sixteenth-century Reformation***—"From the secret place of prayer came the power that shook the world in the Great Reformation. There, with holy calmness, the servants of the Lord set their feet upon the rock of His promises. During the struggle at Augsburg, Luther 'did not pass a day without devoting three hours at least to prayer, and they were hours selected from those the most favorable to study.' In the privacy of his chamber he was heard to pour out his soul before God in words 'full of adoration, fear, and hope, as when one speaks to a friend.' 'I know that Thou art our Father and our God,' he said, 'and that Thou wilt scatter the persecutors of Thy children; for Thou art Thyself endangered with us. All this matter is Thine, and it is only by Thy constraint that we have put our hands to it. Defend us, then, O Father!' " (*The Great Controversy,* p. 210).

# Chapter Eleven

# *The Early and Latter Rain*

***Early rain first***—"We may be sure that when the Holy Spirit is poured out those who did not receive and appreciate the early rain will not see or understand the value of the latter rain" (*Testimonies to Ministers and Gospel Workers*, p. 399).

"As the dew and the rain are given first to cause the seed to germinate, and then to ripen the harvest, so the Holy Spirit is given to carry forward, from one stage to another, the process of spiritual growth....Unless the early showers have done their work, the latter rain can bring no seed to perfection" (*Testimonies to Ministers and Gospel Workers*, p. 506).

"Many have in a great measure failed to receive the former rain. They have not obtained all the benefits that God has thus provided for them. They expect that the lack will be supplied by the latter rain. When the richest abundance of grace shall be bestowed, they intend to open their hearts to receive it. They are making a terrible mistake....Unless we are daily advancing in the exemplification of the active Christian virtues, we shall not recognize the manifestations of the Holy Spirit in the latter rain. It may be falling on hearts all around us, but we shall not discern or receive it" (*Testimonies to Ministers and Gospel Workers*, p. 507).

"If we do not progress, if we do not place ourselves in an attitude to receive both the former and the latter rain, we shall lose our souls, and the responsibility will lie at our own door" (*Testimonies to Ministers and Gospel Workers*, p. 508).

***Power and life***—"The creative energy that called the worlds into existence is in the Word of God. This Word imparts power; it begets life....It transforms the nature and re-creates the soul in the image of God" (*Education*, p. 126).

***The baptism needed***—"What we need is the baptism of the Holy Spirit. Without this, we are no more fitted to go forth to the world than were the disciples after the crucifixion of their Lord. Jesus knew their destitution, and told them to tarry in Jerusalem until they should be endowed with power from on high" (*The Review and Herald*, Feb. 18, 1890).

***Pray for it***—"We should pray as earnestly for the descent of the Holy Spirit as the disciples prayed on the Day of Pentecost. If they needed it at that time, we need it more today" (*Testimonies for the Church*, vol. 5, p. 158).

*Be continually ready*—"I have no specific time of which to speak when the outpouring of the Holy Spirit will take place when the mighty angel will come down from heaven, and unite with the third angel in closing up the work for this world; my message is that our only safety is in being ready for the heavenly refreshing, having our lamps trimmed and burning" (*S.D.A. Bible Commentary*, vol. 7, p. 984; *The Review and Herald*, Mar. 29, 1892).

(Note: Read all of "Pray for the Latter Rain" in *Testimonies to Ministers and Gospel Workers*, pp. 506-512. It is very important.)

- *Chapter Twelve* -

# Seeking God in Prayer

*A wonderful privlege*—"The Lord gives us the privilege of seeking Him individually in earnest prayer, or unburdening our souls to Him, keeping nothing from Him who has invited us, 'Come unto Me, all ye that labor and are heavy-laden, and I will give you rest.' Oh, how grateful we should be that Jesus is willing and able to bear all our infirmities and strengthen and heal all our diseases if it will be for our good and for His glory" (*Medical Ministry*, pp. 16, 17).

*Satan will catch those not seeking Him*—"All who do not earnestly search the Scriptures and submit every desire and purpose of life to that unerring test, all who do not seek God in prayer for a knowledge of His will, will surely wander from the right path and fall under the deception of Satan" (*Testimonies for the Church*, vol. 5, p. 192).

*Brings all needed help*—"We must have less trust in what we ourselves can do, and more trust in what the Lord can do for and through us. You are not engaged in your own work; you are doing the work of God. Surrender your will and way to Him. Make not a single reserve, not a single compromise with self. Know what it is to be free in Christ....

"As you ask the Lord to help you, honor your Saviour by believing that you do receive His blessing. All power, all wisdom, are at our command. We have only to ask.

"Walk continually in the light of God. Meditate day and night upon His character. Then you will see His beauty and rejoice in His goodness. Your heart will glow with a sense of His love. You will be uplifted as if borne by everlasting arms. With the power and light that God imparts, you can comprehend more and accomplish more than you ever before deemed possible" (*The Ministry of Healing*, pp. 513, 514).

# Chapter Thirteen

# *Prayer and Trust*

*A thousand ways*—"Our heavenly Father has a thousand ways to provide for us of which we know nothing. Those who accept the one principle of making the service of God supreme, will find perplexities vanish and a plain path before their feet" (*The Ministry of Healing,* p. 481).

*A lif of trust*—"A life in Christ is a life of restfulness. There may be no ecstasy of feeling, but there should be an abiding, peaceful trust. Your hope is not in yourself; it is in Christ. Your weakness is united to His strength, your ignorance to His wisdom, your frailty to His enduring might. So you are not to look to yourself, not to let the mind dwell upon self, but look to Christ. Let the mind dwell upon His love, upon the beauty, the perfection, of His character. Christ in His self-denial, Christ in His humiliation…Christ in His matchless love this is the subject for the soul's contemplation. It is by loving Him, copying Him, depending wholly upon Him, that you are to be transformed into His likeness" (*Steps to Christ,* pp. 70, 71).

*If we surrender*—"If we surrender our lives to His service, we can never be placed in a position for which God has not made provision. Whatever may be our situation, we have a Guide to direct our way; whatever our perplexities, we have a sure Counselor; whatever our sorrow, bereavement, or loneliness, we have a sympathizing Friend. If in our ignorance we make missteps, Christ does not leave us. His voice, clear and distinct, is heard saying, 'I am the Way, the Truth, and the Life'" (*Christ's Object Lessons,* p. 173).

*Turst youself to Him*—"Worry is blind, and cannot discern the future; but Jesus sees the end from the beginning.…

"In the heart of Christ where reigned perfect harmony with God, there was perfect peace. He was never elated by applause, nor dejected by censure or disappointment. Amid the greatest opposition and the most cruel treatment, He was still of good courage. But many who profess to be His followers have an anxious, troubled heart, because they are afraid to trust themselves with God" (*The Desire of Ages,* p. 330).

*He will help those who trust in Him*—"God will do great things for those who trust in Him. The reason why His professed people have no greater strength is that they trust so much to their own wisdom, and do not give the Lord an opportunity to reveal His power in their behalf. He will help His believing children in every emergency if they will place their entire confidence in Him and faithfully obey Him" (*Patriarchs and Prophets*, p. 493).

# Chapter Fourteen

# Prayer and Reverence

***A sense of God's greatness and presence***—"True reverence for God is inspired by a sense of His infinite greatness and a realization of His presence. With this sense of the Unseen the heart of every child should be deeply impressed" (*Education,* p. 242).

"There is no other way of manifesting reverence so pleasing to Him as obedience to that which He has spoken" (*Education,* p. 244).

***Obedience comes from the heart***—"All true obedience comes from the heart. It was heart work with Christ. And if we consent, He will so identify Himself with our thoughts and aims, so blend our hearts and minds into conformity to His will, that when obeying Him we shall be but carrying out our own impulses.… When we know God as it is our privilege to know Him, our life will be a life of continual obedience. Through an appreciation of the character of Christ, through communion with God, sin will become hateful to us" (*The Desire of Ages,* p. 668).

***With humility and reverence***—"Humility and reverence should characterize the deportment of all who come into the presence of God. In the name of Jesus we may come before Him with confidence, but we must not approach Him with the boldness of presumption, as though He were on a level with ourselves. There are those who address the great and all-powerful and holy God, who dwelleth in light unapproachable, as they would address an equal, or even an inferior.… These should remember that they are in His sight whom seraphim adore, before whom angels veil their faces" (*Patriarchs and Prophets*, p. 252).

***God is at the place of prayer***—"The hour and place of prayer are sacred, because God is there; and as reverence is manifested in attitude and demeanor, the feeling that inspires it will be deepened. 'Holy and reverend is His name,' the psalmist declares. Angels, when they speak that name, veil their faces. With what reverence, then, should we, who are fallen and sinful, take it upon our lips!" (*Gospel Workers,* p. 178).

*"Reverence My sanctuary"*—"To the humble, believing soul, the house of God on earth is the gate of heaven. The song of praise, the prayer, the words spoken by Christ's representatives, are God's appointed agencies to prepare a people for the church above, for that loftier worship into which there can enter nothing that defileth" (*Testimonies for the Church,* vol. 5, p. 491).

*Reverence for His name and Word*—"Reverence should be shown also for the name of God. Never should that name be spoken lightly or thoughtlessly" (*Education,* p. 243).

"We should reverence God's Word. For the printed volume we should show respect, never putting it to common uses, or handling it carelessly" (*Ibid.,* p. 244).

- *Chapter Fifteen* -

# Prayer and Diligence

*Witness of a godly life*—"Character is power. The silent witness of a true, unselfish, godly life carries an almost irresistible influence. By revealing in our own life the character of Christ, we cooperate with Him in the work of saving souls. It is only by revealing in our life His character that we can cooperate with Him. And the wider the sphere of our influence, the more good we may do. When those who profess to serve God follow Christ's example, practicing the principles of the law in their daily life; when every act bears witness that they love God supremely and their neighbor as themselves, then will the church have power to move the world" (*Christ's Object Lessons,* p. 340).

*It radiates from within*—"True character is not shaped from without, and put on; it radiates from within. If we wish to direct others in the path of righteousness, the principles of righteousness must be enshrined in our own hearts" (*The Desire of Ages,* p. 307).

*An argument none can gainsay*—"Our influence upon others depends not so much upon what we say as upon what we are. Men may combat and defy our logic, they may resist our appeals; but a life of disinterested love is an argument they cannot gainsay. A consistent life, characterized by the meekness of Christ, is a power in the world....The word of God, spoken by one who is himself sanctified through it, has a life-giving power that makes it attractive to the hearers, and convicts them that it is a living reality. When one has received the truth in the love of it, he will make this manifest in the persuasion of his manner and the tones of his voice" (*The Desire of Ages,* p. 142).

***Influence of the atmosphere that surrounds us***—"Every soul is surrounded by an atmosphere of its own an atmosphere, it may be, charged with the life-giving power of faith....Or it may be heavy and chill with the gloom of discontent and selfishness.... By the atmosphere surrounding us, every person with whom we come in contact is consciously or unconsciously affected" (*Christ's Object Lessons*, p. 339).

- *Chapter Sixteen* -

# *Prayer and Rejoicing*

***Praise, the atmosphere of heaven***—"The melody of praise is the atmosphere of heaven; and when heaven comes in touch with the earth, there is music and song 'thanksgiving and the voice of melody'" (*Education,* p. 161).

***Jesus met tempation with song***—"With a song, Jesus in His earthly life met temptation. Often when sharp, stinging words were spoken, often when the atmosphere about Him was heavy with gloom, with dissatisfaction, distrust, or oppressive fear, was heard His song of faith and holy cheer" (*Education,* p. 166).

***Study, mediation, and song***—"He studied the Word of God, and His hours of greatest happiness were found when He could turn aside from the scenes of His labors...to hold communion with God.... The early morning often found Him in some secluded place, meditating, searching the Scriptures, or in prayer. With the voice of singing He welcomed the morning light. With songs of thanksgiving He cheered His hours of labor, and brought heaven's gladness to the toilworn and disheartened" (*The Ministry of Healing,* p. 52).

***Use song against discouragement***—"Song is a weapon that we can always use against discouragement. As we thus open the heart to the sunlight of the Saviour's presence, we shall have health and His blessing" (*The Ministry of Healing,* p. 254).

***Gratitude promotes heatlh***—"Nothing tends more to promote health of body and of soul than does a spirit of gratitude and praise. It is a positive duty to resist melancholy, discontented thoughts and feelings as much a duty as it is to pray" (*The Ministry of Healing,* p. 251).

***Cheering the way***—"As the children of Israel, journeying through the wilderness, cheered their way by the music of sacred song, so God bids His children today gladden their pilgrim life. There are few means more effective for fixing His words in the memory than repeating them in song. And such a song has wonderful power" (*Education,* pp. 167, 168).

***Echos from the heavenly choir***—"As our Redeemer leads us to the threshold of the Infinite, flushed with the glory of God, we may catch the themes of praise and thanksgiving from the heavenly choir round about the throne; and as the echo of the angels' song is awakened in our earthly homes, hearts will be drawn closer to the heavenly singers. Heaven's communion begins on earth. We learn here the keynote of its praise" (*Education,* p. 168).

***The song of hope and trust***—"Amidst the deepening shadows of earth's last great crisis, God's light will shine brightest, and the song of hope and trust will be heard in clearest and loftiest strains" (*Education,* p. 166).

*- Chapter Seventeen -*

# The Strength of Prayer

***Strength acquired by***—"Those who seek God in secret telling the Lord their needs and pleading for help, will not plead in vain. 'Thy Father which seeth in secret Himself shall reward thee openly.' As we make Christ our daily companion we shall feel that the powers of an unseen world are all around us; and by looking unto Jesus we shall become assimilated to His image. By beholding we become changed. The character is softened, refined, and ennobled for the heavenly kingdom. The sure result of our intercourse and fellowship with our Lord will be to increase piety, purity, and fervor. There will be a growing intelligence in prayer. We are receiving a divine education, and this is illustrated in a life of diligence and zeal.

"The soul that turns to God for its help, its support, its power, by daily, earnest prayer, will have noble aspirations, clear perceptions of truth and duty, lofty purposes of action, and a continual hungering and thirsting after righteousness. By maintaining a connection with God, we shall be enabled to diffuse to others, through our association with them, the light, the peace, the serenity, that rule in our hearts. The strength acquired in prayer to God, united with persevering effort in training the mind in thoughtfulness and care-taking, prepares one for daily duties and keeps the spirit in peace under all circumstances" (*Thoughts from the Mount of Blessing,* p. 85).

*The source of Christ's strength*—"The strength of Christ was in prayer.…Christ retired to the groves or mountains with the world and everything else shut out. He was alone with His Father. With intense earnestness, He poured out His supplications, and put forth all the strength of His soul in grasping the hand of the Infinite. When new and great trials were before Him, He would steal away to the solitude of the mountains, and pass the entire night in prayer to His heavenly Father.

"As Christ is our example in all things, if we imitate His example in earnest, importunate prayer to God that we may have strength in His name who never yielded to the temptations of Satan to resist the devices of the wily foe, we shall not be overcome by him" (*Sons and Daughters of God,* p. 136).

*Strength and grace*—"Strength and grace can be found in prayer. Sincere love is to be the ruling principle of the heart" (*Testimonies for the Church,* vol. 2, p. 476).

*Preparation for daily duties*—"The strength acquired in prayer to God will prepare us for our daily duties. The temptations to which we are daily exposed make prayer a necessity. In order that we may be kept by the power of God through faith, the desires of the mind should be continually ascending in silent prayer. When we are surrounded by influences calculated to lead us away from God, our petitions for help and strength must be unwearied. Unless this is so, we shall never be successful in breaking down pride and overcoming the power of temptation to sinful indulgences which keep us from the Saviour. The light of truth, sanctifying the life, will discover to the receiver the sinful passions of his heart which are striving for the mastery, and which make it necessary for him to stretch every nerve and exert all his powers to resist Satan that he may conquer through the merits of Christ" (*Messages to Young People,* p. 248).

*Keeps us in peace*—"The strength acquired in prayer to God, united with individual effort in training the mind to thoughtfulness and care-taking, prepares the person for daily duties and keeps the spirit in peace under all circumstances, however trying. The temptations to which we are daily exposed make prayer a necessity. In order that we may be kept by the power of God through faith, the desires of the mind should be continually ascending in silent prayer for help, for light, for strength, for knowledge. But thought and prayer cannot take the place of earnest, faithful improvement of the time. Work and prayer are both required in perfecting Christian character" (*Testimonies for the Church,* vol. 4, p. 459).

***More prayer and less talk***—"Eat less. Engage in physical labor, and devote your mind to spiritual things. Keep your mind from dwelling upon yourself. Cultivate a contented, cheerful spirit. You talk too much upon unimportant things. You gain no spiritual strength from this. If the strength spent in talking were devoted to prayer, you would receive spiritual strength and would make melody in your heart to God" (*Testimonies for the Church*, vol. 2, pp. 434, 435).

***Can be crowded out***—"You need to watch, lest the busy activities of life lead you to neglect prayer when you most need the strength prayer would give. Godliness is in danger of being crowded out of the soul through over-devotion to business. It is a great evil to defraud the soul of the strength and heavenly wisdom which are waiting your demand" (*Testimonies for the Church,* vol. 5, p. 560).

***The Christian's strength***—"The reason why some are restless is that they do not go to the only true source of happiness. They are ever trying to find outside of Christ that enjoyment which is found alone in Him. In Him are no disappointed hopes. Oh, how is the precious privilege of prayer neglected!... Prayer is the strength of the Christian. When alone, he is not alone; he feels the presence of the One who said, 'Lo, I am with you alway'" (*My Life Today,* p. 158).

***Preparation for the crisis***—"The servants of Christ were to prepare no set speech to present when brought to trial. Their preparation was to be made day by day in treasuring up the precious truths of God's word, and through prayer strengthening their faith. When they were brought into trial, the Holy Spirit would bring to their remembrance the very truths that would be needed.

"A daily earnest striving to know God, and Jesus Christ whom He has sent, would bring power and efficiency to the soul. The knowledge obtained by diligent searching of the Scriptures would be flashed into the memory at the right time. But if any had neglected to acquaint themselves with the words of Christ, if they had never tested the power of His grace in trial, they could not expect that the Holy Spirit would bring His words to their remembrance. They were to serve God daily with undivided affection, and then trust Him" (*The Desire of Ages,* p. 355).

***Christ's example is for us***—"Jesus Himself, while He dwelt among men, was often in prayer. Our Saviour identified Himself with our needs and weaknesses, in that He became suppliant, a petitioner, seeking from His Father fresh supplies of strength, that He might come forth braced for duty and trial. He is our example in all things" (*Steps to Christ,* p. 93).

*- Chapter Eighteen -*

# Pray and Work

***Pray and labor***—"You will have to wrestle with difficulties, carry burdens, give advice, plan and execute, constantly looking to God for help. Pray and labor, labor and pray; as pupils in the school of Christ, learn of Jesus" (*Testimonies to Ministers and Gospel Workers,* pp. 498, 499).

***Pray and work***—"We are not to sit in calm expectancy of oppression and tribulation, and fold our hands, doing nothing to avert the evil. Let our united cries be sent up to heaven. Pray and work, and work and pray. But let none act rashly. Learn as never before that you must be meek and lowly in heart" (*Selected Messages,* book 2, pp. 370, 371).

***Pray, work, and believe***—"We must pray and work and believe. The Lord is our efficiency" (*Evangelism,* p. 438).

*- Chapter Nineteen -*

# Ascending Prayer

***He hears the sincere prayer***—"Our heavenly Father waits to bestow upon us the fullness of His blessing. It is our privilege to drink largely at the fountain of boundless love. What a wonder it is that we pray so little! God is ready and willing to hear the sincere prayer of the humblest of His children" (*Steps to Christ,* p. 94).

***Ascends as incense***—"Prayer from a sincere heart ascends as incense before the Lord" (*S.D.A. Bible Commentary*, vol. 6, p. 1059; *The Review and Herald,* May 9, 1893).

***Recorded by the angels***—"We should now acquaint ourselves with God by proving His promises. Angels record every prayer that is earnest and sincere. We should rather dispense with selfish gratifications than neglect communion with God. The deepest poverty, the greatest self-denial, with His approval, is better than riches, honors, ease, and friendship without it. We must take time to pray. If we allow our minds to be absorbed by worldly interests, the Lord may give us time by removing from us our idols of gold, of houses, or of fertile lands" (*The Great Controversy*, p. 622).

**God Himself answers**—"The Bible shows us God in His high and holy place, not in a state of inactivity, not in silence and solitude, but surrounded by ten thousand times ten thousand and thousands of thousands of holy intelligences, all waiting to do His will. Through channels which we cannot discern He is in active communication with every part of His dominion. But it is in this speck of a world, in the souls that He gave His only-begotten Son to save, that His interest and the interest of all heaven is centered. God is bending from His throne to hear the cry of the oppressed. To every sincere prayer He answers, 'Here am I.' He uplifts the distressed and downtrodden. In all our afflictions He is afflicted. In every temptation and every trial the angel of His presence is near to deliver" (*The Desire of Ages*, p. 356).

**Deepens our convictions**—"Our convictions need daily to be reinforced by humble, sincere prayer and reading of the word. While we each have an individuality, while we each should hold our convictions firmly, we must hold them as God's truth and in the strength which God imparts. If we do not, they will be wrung from our grasp" (*Testimonies for the Church*, vol. 6, p. 401).

**When the soul is humbled**—"Let us strive to walk in the light as Christ is in the light. The Lord turned the captivity of Job when he prayed, not only for himself, but for those who were opposing him. When he felt earnestly desirous that the souls that had trespassed against him might be helped, he himself received help. Let us pray, not only for ourselves, but for those who have hurt us, and are continuing to hurt us. Pray, pray, especially in your mind. Give not the Lord rest; for His ears are open to hear sincere, importunate prayers, when the soul is humbled before Him" (*S.D.A. Bible Commentary*, vol. 3, p. 1141; Letter 88, 1906).

**Brought into connection with His mind**—"But if we come to God, feeling helpless and dependent, as we really are, and in humble, trusting faith make known our wants to Him whose knowledge is infinite, who sees everything in creation, and who governs everything by His will and word, He can and will attend to our cry, and will let light shine into our hearts. Through sincere prayer we are brought into connection with the mind of the Infinite. We may have no remarkable evidence at the time that the face of our Redeemer is bending over us in compassion and love, but this is even so. We may not feel His visible touch, but His hand is upon us in love and pitying tenderness" (*Steps to Christ*, p. 97).

***Never lost***—"Let all who are afflicted or unjustly used, cry to God. Turn away from those whose hearts are as steel, and make your requests known to your Maker. Never is one repulsed who comes to Him with a contrite heart. Not one sincere prayer is lost. Amid the anthems of the celestial choir, God hears the cries of the weakest human being. We pour out our heart's desire in our closets, we breathe a prayer as we walk by the way, and our words reach the throne of the Monarch of the universe. They may be inaudible to any human ear, but they cannot die away into silence, nor can they be lost through the activities of business that are going on. Nothing can drown the soul's desire. It rises above the din of the street, above the confusion of the multitude, to the heavenly courts. It is God to whom we are speaking, and our prayer is heard" (*Christ's Object Lessons*, p. 174).

***Prompted by the Spirit***—"The religion that comes from God is the only religion that will lead to God. In order to serve Him aright, we must be born of the divine Spirit. This will purify the heart and renew the mind, giving us a new capacity for knowing and loving God. It will give us a willing obedience to all His requirements. This is true worship. It is the fruit of the working of the Holy Spirit. By the Spirit every sincere prayer is indited, and such prayer is acceptable to God. Wherever a soul reaches out after God, there the Spirit's working is manifest, and God will reveal Himself to that soul. For such worshipers He is seeking. He waits to receive them, and to make them His sons and daughters" (*The Desire of Ages,* p. 189).

***It will be answered***—"Ask, then; ask, and ye shall receive. Ask for humility, wisdom, courage, increase of faith. To every sincere prayer an answer will come. It may not come just as you desire, or at the time you look for it; but it will come in the way and at the time that will best meet your need. The prayers you offer in loneliness, in weariness, in trial, God answers, not always according to your expectations, but always for your good" (*Gospel Workers,* p. 258).

*- Chapter Twenty -*

# The Sincere Prayer

***Praying in sincerity***—"Hence, as we give ourselves to God, and win other souls to Him, we hasten the coming of His kingdom. Only those who devote themselves to His service, saying, 'Here am I; send me' (Isaiah 6:8), to open blind eyes, to turn men 'from darkness to light and from the power of Satan unto God, that they may receive forgiveness of sins and inheritance among them which are sanctified' (Acts 26: 18) they alone pray in sincerity, 'Thy kingdom come'" (*Thoughts from the Mount of Blessing,* p. 109).

***A special characteristic***—"We are in duty bound to draw largely from the treasure house of divine knowledge. God wants us to receive much, in order that we may impart much. He desires us to be channels through which He can impart richly of His grace to the world.

"Let sincerity and faith characterize your prayers. The Lord is willing to do for us 'exceeding abundantly above all that we ask or think.' Ephesians 3:20. Talk it, pray it. Do not talk unbelief. We cannot afford to let Satan see that he has power to darken our countenances and sadden our lives" (*Testimonies for the Church,* vol. 7, p. 273).

***Tested by duty***—"Those who have a natural love for the world and have been remiss in their duty can see their own faults specified in the cases of others who have been reproved. God designs to test the faith of all who claim to be followers of Christ. He will test the sincerity of the prayers of all those who claim to earnestly desire to know their duty. He will make duty plain. He will give all an ample opportunity to develop what is in their hearts. The conflict will be close between self and the grace of God. Self will strive for the mastery and will be opposed to the work of bringing the life and thoughts, the will and affections, into subjection to the will of Christ. Self-denial and the cross stand all along in the pathway to eternal life" (*Testimonies for the Church*, vol. 2, pp. 687, 688).

***Proven by our obedience***—"The sincerity of your prayers will be proved by the vigor of the effort you make to obey all of God's commandments. You may move intelligently, and at every step renounce evil habits and associations, believing that the Lord will renovate your heart by the power of His Spirit.

"Do not excuse your defects of character, but in the grace of Christ overcome them" (*My Life Today,* p. 104).

- Chapter Twenty-one -

# Goals for Prayer

**By imitating Christ's life**—"As God is pure in His sphere, so man is to be pure in his. And he will be pure if Christ is formed within, the hope of glory; for he will imitate Christ's life and reflect His character" (*Gospel Workers,* p. 366).

**The Holy Spirit in our hearts and homes**—"In order to be purified and to remain pure, Seventh-day Adventists must have the Holy Spirit in their hearts and in their homes" (*Testimonies for the Church*, vol. 9, p. 164).

"If ever there was a time when we needed the working of the Spirit of God upon our hearts and lives, it is now. Let us lay hold of this divine power for strength to live a life of holiness and self-surrender" (*Testimonies for the Church*, vol. 9, p. 166).

**All under His control**—"As we work in connection with the Great Teacher, the mental faculties are developed. The conscience is under divine guidance. Christ takes the entire being under His control…. New, rich thoughts come to him [the individual]. Light is given to the intellect, determination to the will, sensitiveness to the conscience, purity to the imagination" (*Testimonies for the Church*, vol. 6, pp. 476, 477).

**Pure in heart here**—"Into the City of God there will enter nothing that defiles. All who are to be dwellers there will here have become pure in heart. In one who is learning of Jesus, there will be manifest a growing distaste for careless manners, unseemly language, and course thought. When Christ abides in the heart, there will be purity and refinement of thought and manner" (*Thoughts from the Mount of Blessing,* pp. 24, 25).

**Beholding Him here**—"If we would enter the City of God, and look upon Jesus in His glory, we must become accustomed to beholding Him with the eye of faith here. The words and character of Christ should be often the subject of our thoughts and our conversation; and each day some time should be especially devoted to prayerful meditation upon these sacred themes" (*Messages to Young People*, p. 114).

**Grow in His likeness**—"Looking unto Jesus we obtain brighter and more distinct views of God, and by beholding we become changed. Goodness, love for our fellowmen, becomes our natural instinct….Growing into His likeness, we enlarge our capacity for knowing God" (*Christ's Object Lessons*, p. 355).

*Live as in His presence now*—"The pure in heart live as in the visible presence of God during the time He apportions them in this world. And they will also see Him face to face in the future immortal state" (*Thoughts from the Mount of Blessing*, p. 27).

*Later face to face*—"We behold the image of God reflected, as in a mirror, in the works of nature and in His dealings with men; but then we shall see Him face to face" (*The Story of Redemption*, p. 432).

*Through study of the Scriptures*—"The Holy Scriptures are the perfect standard of truth, and as such should be given the highest place in education. To obtain an education worthy of the name, we must receive a knowledge of God, the Creator, and of Christ, the Redeemer, as They are revealed in the Sacred Word.

"Every human being, created in the image of God, is endowed with a power akin to that of the Creator individuality, power to think and to do" (*Education*, p. 17).

"As the perfection of His character is dwelt upon, the mind is renewed, and the soul is re-created in the image of God....Higher than the highest human thought can reach is God's ideal for His children. Godliness godlikeness is the goal to be reached" (*Education*, p. 18).

*Experimental knowledge*—"Oh, do we know God as we should? What comfort, what joy, we should have if we were to learn daily the lessons He desires us to learn! We must know Him by an experimental knowledge. It will be profitable for us to spend more time in secret prayer, in becoming personally acquainted with our heavenly Father" (*Medical Ministry*, p. 102).

*Soul re-created in the image of God*—"The knowledge of God as revealed in Christ is the knowledge that all who are saved must have. It is the knowledge that works transformation of character. This knowledge, received, will re-create the soul in the image of God. It will impart to the whole being a spiritual power that is divine" (*The Ministry of Healing*, p. 425).

"As Jesus was in human nature, so God means His followers to be. In His strength we are to live the life of purity and nobility which the Saviour lived" (*The Ministry of Healing*, p. 426).

*Study the prophecies*—The prophecies are to be studied, and the life of Christ compared with the writings of the prophets. He identifies Himself with the prophecies, stating over and over again, They wrote of Me; they testify of Me. The Bible is the only Book giving a positive description of Christ Jesus; and if every human being would study it as his lesson book, and obey it, not a soul would be lost" (*Fundamentals of Christian Education*, p. 382).

***The Word begets life***—"The creative energy that called the worlds into existence is in the Word of God. This Word imparts power; it begets life. Every command is a promise; accepted by the will, received into the soul, it brings with it the life of the Infinite One. It transforms the nature and re-creates the soul in the image of God" (*Education,* p. 126).

***Conversing with God***—"If we keep the Lord ever before us,…we shall have a continual freshness in our religious life. Our prayers will take the form of a conversation with God as we would talk with a friend" (*Christ's Object Lessons*, p. 129).

*- Chapter Twenty-two -*

# Kneeling in Prayer - 1

***Jesus our example***—"May God teach His people how to pray. Let the teachers in our schools and the ministers in our churches, learn daily in the school of Christ. Then they will pray with earnestness, and their requests will be heard and answered. Then the word will be proclaimed with power.

"Both in public and in private worship, it is our privilege to bow on our knees before the Lord when we offer our petitions to Him. Jesus, our example, 'kneeled down, and prayed.' Luke 22:41. Of His disciples it is recorded that they, too, 'kneeled down, and prayed.' Acts 9:40; 20:36; 21:5. Paul declared, 'I bow my knees unto the Father of our Lord Jesus Christ.' Ephesians 3:14. In confessing before God the sins of Israel, Ezra knelt. See Ezra 9:5. Daniel 'kneeled upon his knees three times a day, and prayed, and gave thanks before his God.'" Daniel 6:10.

"True reverence for God is inspired by a sense of His infinite greatness and a realization of His presence. With this sense of the Unseen, every heart should be deeply impressed. The hour and place of prayer are sacred, because God is there; and as reverence is manifested in attitude and demeanor, the feeling that inspires it will be deepened. 'Holy and reverend is His name' (Psalm 111:9), the psalmist declares. Angels, when they speak that name, veil their faces. With what reverence, then, should we, who are fallen and sinful, take it upon our lips!

"Well would it be for old and young to ponder those words of Scripture that show how the place marked by God's special presence should be regarded. 'Put off thy shoes from off thy feet,' He commanded Moses at the burning bush, 'for the place whereon thou standest is holy ground.' Exodus 3:5. Jacob, after beholding the vision of angels, exclaimed, 'The Lord is in this place; and I knew it not.…This is none other but the house of God, and this is the gate of heaven.' Genesis 28:16, 17.

"'The Lord is in His holy temple: let all the earth keep silence before Him.' Habakkuk 2:20" (*Gospel Workers,* pp. 178, 179).

**The humility of Solomon**—"The humility of Solomon at the time he began to bear the burdens of state, when he acknowledged before God, 'I am but a little child' (1 Kings 3:7), his marked love of God, his profound reverence for things divine, his distrust of self, and his exaltation of the infinite Creator of all all these traits of character, so worthy of emulation, were revealed during the services connected with the completion of the temple, when during his dedicatory prayer he knelt in the humble position of a petitioner. Christ's followers today should approach their Maker with humility and awe, through faith in a divine Mediator. The psalmist has declared, 'The Lord is a great God, and a great King above all gods.... O come, let us worship and bow down: let us kneel before the Lord our Maker.' Psalm 95:3-6" (*Prophets and Kings,* pp. 47, 48).

**Solomon's prayer in the assembly**—" 'In the midst of the court' of the temple had been erected 'a brazen scaffold,' or platform, 'five cubits long, and five cubits broad, and three cubits high.' Upon this Solomon stood and with uplifted hands blessed the vast multitude before him. 'And all the congregation of Israel stood.' 2 Chronicles 6:13, 3.

"'Blessed be the Lord God of Israel,' Solomon exclaimed, 'who hath with His hands fulfilled that which He spake with His mouth to my father David, saying,...I have chosen Jerusalem, that My name might be there.' Verses 4-6.

"Solomon then knelt upon the platform, and in the hearing of all the people offered the dedicatory prayer. Lifting his hands toward heaven, while the congregation were bowed with their faces to the ground, the king pleaded: 'Lord God of Israel, there is no God like Thee in the heaven, nor in the earth; which keepest covenant, and showest mercy unto Thy servants, that walk before Thee with all their heart'" (*Prophets and Kings,* pp. 39, 40).

**All bowed during the public prayer**—"King Solomon stood upon a brazen scaffold before the altar and blessed the people. He then knelt down and, with his hands raised upward, poured forth earnest and solemn prayer to God while the congregation were bowed with their faces to the ground. After Solomon had ended his prayer, a miraculous fire came from heaven and consumed the sacrifice" (*The Story of Redemption*, p. 194).

**An example by ministers**—"According to the light that has been given me, it would be pleasing to God for ministers to bow down as soon as they step into the pulpit, and solemnly ask help from God. What impression would that make? There would be solemnity and awe upon their people. Solemnity rests upon the people, and angels of God are brought very near. Ministers should look to God the first thing as they come into the desk, thus saying to all: God is the source of my strength" (*Testimonies for the Church*, vol. 2, p. 613).

*Every knee should bow*—"When the minister enters, it should be with dignified, solemn mien. He should bow down in silent prayer as soon as he steps into the pulpit, and earnestly ask help of God. What an impression this will make! There will be solemnity and awe upon the people. Their minister is communing with God; he is committing himself to God before he dares to stand before the people. Solemnity rests upon all, and angels of God are brought very near. Every one of the congregation, also, who fears God should with bowed head unite in silent prayer with him that God may grace the meeting with His presence and give power to His truth proclaimed from human lips. When the meeting is opened by prayer, every knee should bow in the presence of the Holy One, and every heart should ascend to God in silent devotion. The prayers of faithful worshipers will be heard, and the ministry of the word will prove effectual. The lifeless attitude of the worshipers in the house of God is one great reason why the ministry is not more productive of good. The melody of song, poured forth from many hearts in clear, distinct utterance, is one of God's instrumentalities in the work of saving souls. All the service should be conducted with solemnity and awe, as if in the visible presence of the Master of assemblies" (*Testimonies for the Church,* vol. 5, pp. 492, 493).

*A natural position*—"Many feel that praying injures their vocal organs more than talking. This is in consequence of the unnatural position of the body, and the manner of holding the head. They can stand and talk, and not feel injured. The position in prayer should be perfectly natural" (*Testimonies for the Church*, vol. 2, p. 617).

*How Ezra prayed*—"At the time of the evening sacrifice Ezra rose, and, once more rending his garment and his mantle, he fell upon his knees and unburdened his soul in supplication to Heaven. Spreading out his hands unto the Lord, he exclaimed, "O my God, I am ashamed and blush to lift up my face to Thee, my God: for our iniquities are increased over our head, and our trespass is grown up unto the heavens" (*Prophets and Kings,* pp. 620, 621).

*Jacob's prayer*—"Solitary and unprotected, Jacob bowed in deep distress upon the earth. It was midnight. All that made life dear to him were at a distance, exposed to danger and death. Bitterest of all was the thought that it was his own sin which had brought this peril upon the innocent. With earnest cries and tears he made his prayer before God" (*Patriarchs and Prophets*, pp. 196, 197).

*Prostrate in prayer*—"Where He [Christ] is bowed in lowliness upon the stony ground, suddenly the heavens open, the golden gates of the city of God are thrown wide, and holy radiance descends upon the mount, enshrouding the Saviour's form. Divinity from within flashes through humanity, and meets the glory coming from above. Arising from His prostrate position, Christ stands in godlike majesty. The soul agony is gone. His countenance now shines 'as the sun,' and His garments are 'white as the light'" (*The Desire of Ages,* p. 421).

*On the ground*—"Behold Him contemplating the price to be paid for the human soul. In His agony He clings to the cold ground, as if to prevent Himself from being drawn farther from God. The chilling dew of night falls upon His prostrate form, but He heeds it not. From His pale lips comes the bitter cry, 'O My Father, if it be possible, let this cup pass from Me.' Yet even now He adds, 'Nevertheless not as I will, but as Thou wilt'" (*The Desire of Ages,* p. 687).

*Falling prostrate*—"Turning away, Jesus sought again His retreat, and fell prostrate, overcome by the horror of a great darkness. The humanity of the Son of God trembled in that trying hour. He prayed not now for His disciples that their faith might not fail, but for His own tempted, agonized soul. The awful moment had come that moment which was to decide the destiny of the world" (*The Desire of Ages,* p. 690).

*The example of Daniel*—"Now when Daniel knew that the writing was signed, he went into his house; and his windows being open in his chamber toward Jerusalem, he kneeled upon his knees three times a day, and prayed, and gave thanks before his God, as he did aforetime" (Daniel 6:10).

*Your knees are to bow*—"Your mind was given that you might understand how to work. Your eyes were given that you might be keen to discern your God-given opportunities. Your ears are to listen for the commands of God. Your knees are to bow three times a day in heartfelt prayer. Your feet are to run in the way of God's commandments. Thought, effort, talent, should be put into exercise, that you may be prepared to graduate into the school above and hear from the lips of One who has overcome all temptations in our behalf the words: 'To him that overcometh will I grant to sit with Me in My throne, even as I also overcame, and am set down with My Father in His throne'" (*Testimonies for the Church,* vol. 6, p. 298).

*The example of Paul*—"And when he had thus spoken, he kneeled down, and prayed with them all. And they all wept sore, and fell on Paul's neck, and kissed him, sorrowing most of all for the words which he spake, that they should see his face no more. And they accompanied him unto the ship" (Acts 20:36-38).

***The example of Peter***—"The apostle's heart was touched with sympathy as he beheld their sorrow. Then, directing that the weeping friends be sent from the room, he kneeled down and prayed fervently to God to restore Dorcas to life and health. Turning to the body, he said, 'Tabitha, arise. And she opened her eyes: and when she saw Peter, she sat up.' Dorcas had been of great service to the church, and God saw fit to bring her back from the land of the enemy, that her skill and energy might still be a blessing to others, and also that by this manifestation of His power the cause of Christ might be strengthened" (*The Acts of the Apostles,* p. 132).

*- Chapter Twenty-three -*

# Kneeling in Prayer - 2

***Preparation for ministering***—"Be waiting, watching for every opportunity to present the truth, familiar with the prophecies, familiar with the lessons of Christ. But do not trust in well-prepared arguments. Argument alone is not enough. God must be sought on your knees; you must go forth to meet the people through the power and influence of His Spirit" (*S.D.A. Bible Commentary*, vol. 2, p. 1004; *The Review and Herald,* July 1, 1884).

***A deep truth for God's people in these last days***—"I have received letters questioning me in regard to the proper attitude to be taken by a person offering prayer to the Sovereign of the universe. Where have our brethren obtained the idea that they should stand upon their feet when praying to God? One who has been educated for about five years in Battle Creek was asked to lead in prayer before Sister White should speak to the people. But as I beheld him standing upright upon his feet while his lips were about to open in prayer to God, my soul was stirred within me to give him an open rebuke. Calling him by name, I said, 'Get down upon your knees.' This is the proper position always.

"'And he was withdrawn from them about a stone's cast, and kneeled down, and prayed' (Luke 22:41).

"'Peter put them all forth, and kneeled down, and prayed; and turning him to the body said, Tabitha, arise. And she opened her eyes: and when she saw Peter, she sat up' (Acts 9:40).

"'They stoned Stephen, calling upon God, and saying, Lord Jesus, receive my spirit. And he kneeled down, and cried with a loud voice, Lord, lay not this sin to their charge. And when he had said this, he fell asleep' (Acts 7:59, 60).

"'When he had thus spoken, he kneeled down, and prayed with them all' (Acts 20:36).

"'When we had accomplished those days, we departed and went our way; and they all brought us on our way, with wives and children, till we were out of the city: and we kneeled down on the shore, and prayed' (Acts 21:5).

"'At the evening sacrifice I arose up from my heaviness; and having rent my garment and my mantle, I fell upon my knees, and spread out my hands unto the Lord my God, and said, O my God, I am ashamed and blush to lift up my face to thee, my God: for our iniquities are increased over our head, and our trespass is grown up unto the heavens' (Ezra 9:5, 6).

"'O come, let us worship and bow down: let us kneel before the Lord our maker' (Psalms 95:6).

"'For this cause I bow my knees unto the Father of our Lord Jesus Christ' (Ephesians 3:14). And this whole chapter will, if the heart is receptive, be as precious a lesson as we can learn.

"To bow down when in prayer to God is the proper attitude to occupy. This act of worship was required of the three Hebrew captives of Babylon.... But such an act was homage to be rendered to God alone the Sovereign of the world, the Ruler of the universe; and these three Hebrews refused to give such honor to any idol even though composed of pure gold. In doing so, they would, to all intents and purposes, be bowing to the king of Babylon. Refusing to do as the king had commanded, they suffered the penalty, and were cast into the burning fiery furnace. But Christ came in person and walked with them through the fire, and they received no harm.

"Both in public and private worship it is our duty to bow down upon our knees before God when we offer our petitions to Him. This act shows our dependence upon God.

"At the dedication of the Temple, Solomon stood facing the altar. In the court of the Temple was a brazen scaffold or platform, and after ascending this, he stood and lifted up his hands to heaven, and blessed the immense congregation of Israel, and all the congregation of Israel stood....

"'For Solomon had made a brasen scaffold, of five cubits long, and five cubits broad, and three cubits high, and had set it in the midst of the court: and upon it he stood, and kneeled down upon his knees before all the congregation of Israel, and spread forth his hands toward heaven' (2 Chronicles 6:13).

"The lengthy prayer which he then offered was appropriate for the occasion. It was inspired of God, breathing the sentiments of the loftiest piety blended with the deepest humility.

"I present these proof texts with the inquiry, 'Where did Brother H obtain his education? At Battle Creek. Is it possible that with all the light that God has given to His people on the subject of reverence, that ministers, principals, and teachers in our schools, by precept and example, teach young men to stand erect in devotion as did the Pharisees? Shall we look upon this as significant of their self-sufficiency and self-importance? Are these traits to become conspicuous?

"'And he spake this parable unto certain which trusted in themselves that they were righteous, and despised others: Two men went up into the temple to pray; the one a Pharisee, and the other a publican. The Pharisee stood and prayed thus with himself, God, I thank thee, that I am not as other men are, extortioners, unjust, adulterers, or even as this publican. I fast twice in the week, I give tithes of all I possess' (Luke 18:9-12). Mark you, it was the self-righteous Pharisee who was not in a position of humility and reverence before God; but standing in his haughty self-sufficiency, he told the Lord all his good deeds. 'The Pharisee stood and prayed thus with himself' (Luke 18:11); and his prayer reached no higher than himself.

"'And the publican, standing afar off, would not lift up so much as his eyes unto heaven, but smote upon his breast, saying, God be merciful to me a sinner. I tell you, this man went down to his house justified rather than the other: for every one that exalteth himself shall be abased; and he that humbleth himself shall be exalted' (Luke 18:13, 14).

"We hope that our brethren will not manifest less reverence and awe as they approach the only true and living God than the heathen manifest for their idol deities, or these people will be our judges in the day of final decision. I would speak to all who occupy the place of teachers in our schools. Men and women, do not dishonor God by your irreverence and pomposity. Do not stand up in your Pharisaism and offer your prayers to God. Mistrust your own strength. Depend not in it; but often bow down on your knees before God, and worship Him.

"And when you assemble to worship God, be sure and bow your knees before Him. Let this act testify that the whole soul, body, and spirit are in subjection to the Spirit of truth. Who have searched the Word closely for examples and direction in this respect? Whom can we trust as teachers in our schools in America and foreign countries? After years of study shall students return to their own country with perverted ideas of the respect and honor and reverence that should be given to God, and feel under no obligation to honor the men of gray hairs, the men of experience, the chosen servants of God who have been connected with the work of God through almost all the years of their life? I advise all who attend the schools in America or in any other place, do not catch the spirit of irreverence. Be sure you understand for yourself what kind of education you need, that you may educate others to obtain a fitness of character that will stand the test that is soon to be brought upon all who live upon the earth. Keep company with the soundest Christians. Choose not the pretentious instructors or pupils, but those who show the deepest piety, those who have a spirit of intelligence in the things of God.

"We are living in perilous times. Seventh-day Adventists are professedly the commandment-keeping people of God; but they are losing their devotional spirit. This spirit of reverence for God teaches men how to approach their Maker with sacredness and awe through faith, not in themselves, but in a Mediator. Thus man is kept fast, under whatever circumstances he is placed. Man must come on bended knee, as a subject of grace, a suppliant at the footstool of mercy. And as he receives daily mercies at the hand of God, he is ever to cherish gratitude in his heart, and give expression to it in the words of thanksgiving and praise for these unmerited favors. Angels have been guarding his pathway through all his life, and many of the snares he has been delivered from he has not seen. And for this guardianship and watchcare by eyes that never slumber and never sleep, he is to recognize in every prayer the service of God for him.

"All should lean upon God in their helplessness and daily necessity. They should keep humble, watchful, and prayerful. Praise and thanksgiving should flow forth in gratitude and sincere love for God.

"In the assembly of the upright and in the congregation should they praise the Most High God. All who have a sense of their vital connection with God should stand before the Lord as witnesses for Him, giving expression of the love. the mercies, and the goodness of God. Let the words be sincere, simple, earnest, intelligent, the heart burning with the love of God, the lips sanctified to His glory not only to make known the mercies of God in the assembly of the saints but to be His witnesses in every place. The inhabitants of the earth are to know that He is God, the only true and living God.

"There should be an intelligent knowledge of how to come to God in reverence and godly fear with devotional love. There is a growing lack of reverence for our Maker, a growing disregard of His greatness and His majesty. But God is speaking to us in these last days. We hear His voice in the storm, in the rolling thunder. We hear of the calamities He permits in the earthquakes, the breaking forth of waters, and the destructive elements sweeping all before them. We hear of ships going down in the tempestuous ocean. God speaks to families who have refused to recognize Him, sometimes in the whirlwind and storm, sometimes face to face as He talked with Moses. Again He whispers His love to the little trusting child and to the gray-haired sire in his dotage. And earthly wisdom has a wisdom as it beholds the unseen.

"When the still small voice which succeeds the whirlwind and the tempest that moves the rocks out of position, is heard, let all cover their face, for God is very near. Let them hide themselves in Jesus Christ; for He is their hiding place. The cleft of the rock is hidden with His own pierced hand while the humble seeker waits in bowed attitude to hear what saith the Lord unto His servant" (*Selected Messages,* book 2, pp. 311-316).

# Chapter Twenty-four

# When We Need Not Kneel

***The way always open***—"We cannot always be on our knees in prayer, but the way to the mercy seat is always open. While engaged in active labor, we may ask for help; and we are promised by One who will not deceive us, 'Ye shall receive.' The Christian can and will find time to pray. Daniel was a statesman; heavy responsibilities rested upon him; yet three times a day he sought God, and the Lord gave him the Holy Spirit. So today men may resort to the sacred pavilion of the Most High and feel the assurance of His promise, 'My people shall dwell in a peaceable habitation, and in sure dwellings, and in quiet resting places.' Isaiah 32:18. All who really desire it can find a place for communion with God, where no ear can hear but the one open to the cries of the helpless, distressed, and needy the One who notices even the fall of the little sparrow. He says, 'Ye are of more value than many sparrows.' Matthew 10:31" (*Counsels on Health*, pp. 423, 424).

***In business and in transit***—"There is no time or place in which it is inappropriate to offer up a petition to God....In the crowds of the street, in the midst of a business engagement, we may send up a petition to God, and plead for divine guidance, as did Nehemiah when he made his request before King Artaxerxes" (*Selected Messages,* book 2, p. 316).

***In labor or on the street***—"It is a wonderful thing that we can pray effectually; that unworthy, erring mortals possess the power of offering their requests to God. What higher power can man desire than this, to be linked with the infinite God? Feeble, sinful man has the privilege of speaking to his Maker. We may utter words that reach the throne of the Monarch of the universe. We may speak with Jesus as we walk by the way, and He says, I am at thy right hand.

"We may commune with God in our hearts; we may walk in companionship with Christ. When engaged in our daily labor, we may breathe out our heart's desire, inaudible to any human ear; but that word cannot die away into silence, nor can it be lost. Nothing can drown the soul's desire. It rises above the din of the street, above the noise of machinery. It is God to whom we are speaking, and our prayer is heard.

"Ask, then; ask, and ye shall receive. Ask for humility, wisdom, courage, increase of faith. To every sincere prayer an answer will come. It may not come just as you desire, or at the time you look for it; but it will come in the way and at the time that will best meet your need. The prayers you offer in loneliness, in weariness, in trial, God answers, not always according to your expectations, but always for your good" (*Gospel Workers,* p. 258).

***All through the day***—"The reason why so many are left to themselves in places of temptation is that they do not set the Lord always before them. When we permit our communion with God to be broken, our defense is departed from us. Not all your good purposes and good intentions will enable you to withstand evil. You must be men and women of prayer. Your petitions must not be faint, occasional, and fitful, but earnest, persevering, and constant. It is not always necessary to bow upon your knees in order to pray. Cultivate the habit of talking with the Saviour when you are alone, when you are walking, and when you are busy with your daily labor. Let the heart be continually uplifted in silent petition for help, for light, for strength, for knowledge. Let every breath be a prayer" (*The Ministry of Healing,* pp. 510, 511).

***Thoughts always upward***—"In the work of heart-keeping we must be instant in prayer, unwearied in petitioning the throne of grace for assistance. Those who take the name of Christian should come to God in earnestness and humility, pleading for help. The Saviour has told us to pray without ceasing. The Christian can not always be in the position of prayer, but his thoughts and desires can always be upward. Our self-confidence would vanish, did we talk less and pray more" (*S.D.A. Bible Commentary,* vol. 3, p. 1157; *The Youth's Instructor,* Mar. 5, 1903).

***When tempted***—"The way to the throne of God is always open. You cannot always be on your knees in prayer, but your silent petitions may constantly ascend to God for strength and guidance. When tempted, as you will be, you may flee to the secret place of the Most High. His everlasting arms will be underneath you. Let these words cheer you, 'Thou hast a few names even in Sardis which have not defiled their garments; and they shall walk with Me in white: for they are worthy.' Revelation 3:4" (*Counsels on Health*, p. 362).

***During business***—"Wherever we are, whatever our employment, our hearts are to be uplifted to God in prayer. This is being instant in prayer. We need not wait until we can bow upon our knees, before we pray. On one occasion, when Nehemiah came in before the king, the king asked why he looked so sad, and what request he had to make. But Nehemiah dared not answer at once. Important interests were at stake. The fate of a nation hung upon the impression that should then be made upon the monarch's mind; and Nehemiah darted up a prayer to the God of heaven, before he dared to answer the king. The result was that he obtained all that he asked or even desired" (*S.D.A. Bible Commentary*, vol. 3, p. 1136; *Historical Sketches of the Foreign Missions of the Seventh-day Adventists,* p. 144).

*Working outdoors*—"If all our workers were so situated that they could spend a few hours each day in outdoor labor, and felt free to do this, it would be a blessing to them; they would be able to discharge more successfully the duties of their calling. If they have not time for complete relaxation, they could be planning and praying while at work with their hands, and could return to the labor refreshed in body and spirit" (*Counsels on Health*, p. 564).

*Often uplifted*—"Pray in your closet, and as you go about your daily labor let your heart be often uplifted to God. It was thus that Enoch walked with God. These silent prayers rise like precious incense before the throne of grace. Satan cannot overcome him whose heart is thus stayed upon God" (*Steps to Christ,* pp. 98, 99).

*Momentarily receive supplies*—"Christ is ever sending messages to those who listen for His voice....

"Satan is ever seeking to impress and control the mind, and none of us are safe except as we have a constant connection with God. We must momentarily receive supplies from heaven, and if we would be kept by the power of God we must be obedient to all His requirements.

"The condition of your bearing fruit is that you abide in the living Vine....

"All your good purposes and good intentions will not enable you to withstand the test of temptation. You must be men of prayer. Your petitions must be not faint, occasional, and fitful, but earnest, persevering, and constant. It is not necessary to be alone, or to bow upon your knees, to pray; but in the midst of your labor your souls may be often uplifted to God, taking hold upon His strength; then you will be men of high and holy purpose, of noble integrity, who will not for any consideration be swayed from truth, right, and justice" (*Testimonies for the Church,* vol. 4, pp. 542, 543).

*Wherever we may be*—"We must pray constantly, with a humble mind and a meek and lowly spirit. We need not wait for an opportunity to kneel before God. We can pray and talk with the Lord wherever we may be" (*Selected Messages*, book 3, p. 266).

*During the closing appeal prayer in meetings*—(Read *Selected Messages*, book 3, pages 267-270. The closing prayer is the only public worship prayer/prayer in a worship service to be offered standing.)

*Praying while standing*—(Only time in Scripture: Matthew 6:5 the prayer of the hypocrites; Luke 18:11-12 the prayer of the proud Pharisee; Luke 18:13-14 the prayer of an ignorant worldling initially coming to God. Compare with *The Desire of Ages*, p. 495; *Testimonies for the Church*, vol. 1, p. 416; *Steps to Christ*, p. 31; *Christ's Object Lessons,* pp. 150-159.)

***Did Solomon stand to pray?***—Did Solomon stand to pray during his prayer at the dedication of the temple? If so, this would be the only standing public worship prayer in the Bible. 1 Kings 8:22 does not tell the whole story. Read *Patriarchs and Prophets*, pp. 39, 40 and *The Story of Redemption*, p. 194. First, Solomon stood and all the congregation with him and he blessed the people (1 Kings 8:14). Then he knelt to pray while the people fell on their faces (*Patriarchs and Prophets*, pp. 39, 40; *The Story of Redemption*, p. 194), and he uttered that public worship prayer. The prayer is recorded in 2 Chronicles 6 and 1 Kings 8. When ended, he and the people arose to their feet (read 1 Kings 8:54-55), and then while standing he blessed the people again and encouraged them to obey God (1 Kings 8:55-61).

- *Chapter Twenty-five* -

# *The Promises of Prayer*

***The purpose of God's promises***—"God has placed the promises in His Word to lead us to have faith in Him. In these promises He draws back the veil from eternity, giving us a glimpse of the far more exceeding and eternal weight of glory which awaits the overcomer" (*My Life Today*, p. 338).

***Answers will come***—"The simple prayers indited by the Holy Spirit will ascend through the gates ajar, the open door which Christ has declared: I have opened, and no man can shut. These prayers, mingled with the incense of the perfection of Christ, will ascend as fragrance to the Father, and answers will come" (*Testimonies for the Church*, vol. 6, p. 467).

***There is abundant help***—"The fact that you have been baptized in the name of the Father, the Son, and the Holy Spirit is an assurance that, if you will claim Their help, these Powers will help you in every emergency" (*Testimonies for the Church*, vol. 6, p. 99).

***Angels will be sent***—"The guardianship of the heavenly host is granted to all who will work in God's ways and follow His plans. We may in earnest, contrite prayer call the heavenly helpers to our side. Invisible armies of light and power will work with the humble, meek, and lowly one" (*Selected Messages*, book 1, p. 97).

*Help for every emergency*—"Toilers in the busy walks of life, crowded and almost overwhelmed with perplexity, can send up a petition to God for divine guidance. Travelers by sea and land, when threatened with some great danger, can thus commit themselves to Heaven's protection. In times of sudden difficulty or peril the heart may send up its cry for help to One who has pledged Himself to come to the aid of His faithful, believing ones whenever they call upon Him" (*Prophets and Kings,* pp. 631, 632).

*An unchanging love*—"If one who daily communes with God errs from the path, if he turns a moment from looking steadfastly unto Jesus, it is not because he sins willfully; for when he sees his mistake, he turns again, and fastens his eyes upon Jesus, and the fact that he has erred, does not make him less dear to the heart of God" (*The Review and Herald*, May 12, 1896).

*Claim by faith every promise*—"Is Jesus true? Does He mean what He says? Answer decidedly, Yes, every word. Then if you have settled this, by faith claim every promise that He has made, and receive the blessing; for this acceptance by faith gives life to the soul. You may believe that Jesus is true to you, even though you feel yourself to be the weakest and most unworthy of His children" (*Testimonies to Ministers and Gospel Workers,* p. 517).

*- Chapter Twenty-six -*

# Private Prayers

*Private prayer is different*—"[In public meetings] upon common occasions there should not be prayer of more than ten minutes' duration. After there has been a change of position, and the exercise of singing or exhortation has relieved the sameness, then, if any feel the burden of prayer, let them pray.

"All should feel it a Christian duty to pray short. Tell the Lord just what you want, without going all over the world. In private prayer all have the privilege of praying as long as they desire and of being as explicit as they please. They can pray for all their relatives and friends. The closet is the place to tell all their private difficulties, and trials, and temptations. A common meeting to worship God is not the place to open the privacies of the heart.

"What is the object of assembling together? Is it to inform God, to instruct Him by telling Him all we know in prayer?" (*Testimonies for the Church,* vol. 2, p. 578).

**All are essential**—"Private prayer, family prayer, prayer in public gatherings for the worship of God all are essential. And we are to live our prayers. We are to cooperate with Christ in His work" (*Testimonies for the Church,* vol. 7, p. 239).

**Prayer meeting killers**—"There are some, I fear, who do not take their troubles to God in private prayer, but reserve them for the prayer meeting, and there do up their praying for several days. Such may be named conference and prayer meeting killers. They emit no light; they edify no one. Their cold, frozen prayers and long, backslidden testimonies cast a shadow. All are glad when they get through, and it is almost impossible to throw off the chill and darkness which their prayers and exhortations bring into the meeting. From the light which I have received, our meetings should be spiritual and social, and not too long. Reserve, pride, vanity, and fear of man should be left at home. Little differences and prejudices should not be taken with us to these meetings. As in a united family, simplicity, meekness, confidence, and love should exist in the hearts of brethren and sisters who meet to be refreshed and invigorated by bringing their lights together" (*Testimonies for the Church,* vol. 2, pp. 578, 579).

**Private prayer not public**—"The Pharisees had stated hours for prayer; and when, as often came to pass, they were abroad at the appointed time, they would pause wherever they might be perhaps in the street or the market place, amid the hurrying throngs of men and there in a loud voice rehearse their formal prayers. Such worship, offered merely for self-glorification, called forth unsparing rebuke from Jesus. He did not, however, discountenance public prayer, for He Himself prayed with His disciples and in the presence of the multitude. But He teaches that private prayer is not to be made public. In secret devotion our prayers are to reach the ears of none but the prayer-hearing God. No curious ear is to receive the burden of such petitions.

" 'When thou prayest, enter into thy closet.' Have a place for secret prayer. Jesus had select places for communion with God, and so should we. We need often to retire to some spot, however humble, where we can be alone with God.

" 'Pray to thy Father which is in secret.' In the name of Jesus we may come into God's presence with the confidence of a child. No man is needed to act as a mediator. Through Jesus we may open our hearts to God as to one who knows and loves us.

"In the secret place of prayer, where no eye but God's can see, no ear but His can hear, we may pour out our most hidden desires and longings to the Father of infinite pity, and in the hush and silence of the soul that voice which never fails to answer the cry of human need will speak to our hearts" (*Thoughts from the Mount of Blessing,* pp. 83, 84).

# Chapter Twenty-seven

# Safeguards for the Future

**Thus saith the Lord** —"When Satan presses his suggestions upon our minds, we may, if we cherish a 'Thus saith the Lord,' be drawn into the secret pavilion of the Most High" (*Testimonies for the Church*, vol. 6, p. 393).

**Knowledge of the truth a defense**—"Those who are earnestly seeking a knowledge of the truth and are striving to purify their souls through obedience, thus doing what they can to prepare for the conflict, will find, in the God of truth, a sure defense. 'Because thou hast kept the word of My patience, I also will keep thee' (Revelation 3:10), is the Saviour's promise. He would sooner send every angel out of heaven to protect His people than leave one soul that trusts in Him to be overcome by Satan" (*The Great Controversy*, p. 560).

**The Scriptures a safeguard**—"The people of God are directed to the Scriptures as their safeguard against the influence of false teachers and the delusive power of spirits of darkness. Satan employs every possible device to prevent men from obtaining a knowledge of the Bible; for its plain utterances reveal his deceptions....The last great delusion is soon to open before us....So closely will the counterfeit resemble the true that it will be impossible to distinguish between them except by the Holy Scriptures. By their testimony every statement and every miracle must be tested....

"None but those who have fortified the mind with the truths of the Bible will stand through the last great conflict" (*The Great Controversy*, pp. 593, 594).

**Remembering what is there**—"Jesus promised His disciples: 'The Comforter, which is the Holy Ghost, whom the Father will send in My name, He shall teach you all things, and bring all things to your remembrance, whatsoever I have said unto you.' But the teachings of Christ must previously have been stored in the mind in order for the Spirit of God to bring them to our remembrance in the time of peril" (*The Great Controversy*, p. 600).

**Flashed into the memory**—"A daily, earnest striving to know God, and Jesus Christ whom He has sent, would bring power and efficiency to the soul. The knowledge obtained by diligent searching of the Scriptures would be flashed into the memory at the right time. But if any had neglected to acquaint themselves with the words of Christ...they could not expect that the Holy Spirit would bring His words to their remembrance. They were to serve God daily with undivided affection, and then trust Him" (*The Desire of Ages,* p. 355).

***"It is written"***—"God's tried and tested people are to take their stand on the living Word: 'It is written'" (*Testimonies for the Church,* vol. 9, p. 16).

- Chapter Twenty-eight -

# Be Much in Secret Prayer

***Be much in***—"We should be much in secret prayer. Christ is the vine, ye are the branches. And if we would grow and flourish, we must continually draw sap and nourishment from the Living Vine; for separated from the Vine we have no strength.

"I asked the angel why there was no more faith and power in Israel. He said, 'Ye let go of the arm of the Lord too soon. Press your petitions to the throne, and hold on by strong faith. The promises are sure. Believe ye receive the things ye ask for, and ye shall have them'" (*Early Writings,* p. 73).

***How precious!***—"When the heart is divided, dwelling principally upon things of the world, and but little upon the things of God, there can be no special increase of spiritual strength. Worldly enterprises claim the larger share of the mind, calling into exercise its powers; therefore in this direction there is strength and power to claim more and more of the interest and affections, while less and less is reserved to devote to God. It is impossible for the soul to flourish while prayer is not a special exercise of the mind. Family or public prayer alone is not sufficient. Secret prayer is very important; in solitude the soul is laid bare to the inspecting eye of God, and every motive is scrutinized. Secret prayer! How precious! The soul communing with God! Secret prayer is to be heard only by the prayer-hearing God. No curious ear is to receive the burden of such petitions. In secret prayer the soul is free from surrounding influences, free from excitement. Calmly, yet fervently, will it reach out after God. Secret prayer is frequently perverted, and its sweet designs lost, by loud vocal prayer. Instead of the calm, quiet trust and faith in God, the soul drawn out in low, humble tones, the voice is raised to a loud pitch, and excitement is encouraged, and secret prayer loses its softening, sacred influence. There is a storm of feeling, a storm of words, making it impossible to discern the still, small voice that speaks to the soul while engaged in its secret, true, heartfelt devotion. Secret prayer, properly carried out, is productive of great good. But prayer which is made public to the entire family and neighborhood is not secret prayer, even though thought to be, and divine strength is not received from it. Sweet and abiding will be the influence emanating from Him who seeth in secret, whose ear is open to answer the prayer arising from the heart. By calm, simple faith the soul holds communion with God and gathers to itself divine rays of light to strengthen and sustain it to endure the conflicts of Satan. God is our tower of strength" (*Testimonies for the Church*, vol. 2, pp. 189, 190).

**Brings its reward**—"Amid the perils of these last days, the only safety of the youth lies in ever-increasing watchfulness and prayer. The youth who finds his joy in reading the word of God, and in the hour of prayer, will be constantly refreshed by drafts from the fountain of life. He will attain a height of moral excellence and a breadth of thought of which others cannot conceive. Communion with God encourages good thoughts, noble aspirations, clear perceptions of truth, and lofty purposes of action. Those who thus connect themselves with God are acknowledged by Him as His sons and daughters. They are constantly reaching higher and still higher, obtaining clearer views of God and of eternity, until the Lord makes them channels of light and wisdom to the world.

"But prayer is not understood as it should be. Our prayers are not to inform God of something He does not know. The Lord is acquainted with the secrets of every soul. Our prayers need not be long and loud. God reads the hidden thoughts. We may pray in secret, and He who sees in secret will hear, and will reward us openly.

"The prayers that are offered to God to tell Him of all our wretchedness, when we do not feel wretched at all, are the prayers of hypocrisy. It is the contrite prayer that the Lord regards. 'For thus saith the high and lofty One that inhabiteth eternity, whose name is Holy; I dwell in the high and holy place, and with him also that is of a contrite and humble spirit, to revive the spirit of the humble, and to revive the heart of the contrite ones.'

"Prayer is not intended to work any change in God; it brings us into harmony with God. It does not take the place of duty. Prayer offered ever so often and ever so earnestly will never be accepted by God in the place of our tithe. Prayer will not pay our debts to God...." (*Messages to Young People*, pp. 247, 248).

**The beginning of evil**—"The very beginning of the evil was a neglect of watchfulness and secret prayer, then came a neglect of other religious duties, and thus the way was opened for all the sins that followed. Every Christian will be assailed by the allurements of the world, the clamors of the carnal nature, and the direct temptations of Satan. No one is safe. No matter what our experience has been, no matter how high our station, we need to watch and pray continually. We must be daily controlled by the Spirit of God or we are controlled by Satan" (*Testimonies for the Church,* vol. 5, p. 102).

*Amusements disqualify for*—"The idea is to have a general high time. Their amusements commence in folly and end in vanity. Our gatherings should be so conducted, and we should so conduct ourselves, that when we return to our homes we can have a conscience void of offense toward God and man; a consciousness that we have not wounded or injured in any manner those with whom we have been associated, or had an injurious influence over them....

"Any amusement in which you can engage asking the blessing of God upon it in faith will not be dangerous. But any amusement which disqualifies you for secret prayer, for devotion at the altar of prayer, or for taking part in the prayer meeting, is not safe, but dangerous" (*Counsels to Parents, Teachers, and Students,* p. 336).

*Keyed to dedication and obedience*—"Our Creator demands our supreme devotion, our first allegiance. Anything which tends to abate our love for God, or to interfere with the service due Him, becomes thereby an idol. With some their lands, their houses, their merchandise, are the idols. Business enterprises are prosecuted with zeal and energy, while the service of God is made a secondary consideration. Family worship is neglected, secret prayer forgotten. Many claim to deal justly with their fellow-men, and seem to feel that in so doing they discharge their whole duty. But it is not enough to keep the last six commandments of the Decalogue. We are to love the Lord our God with all the heart. Nothing short of obedience to every precept...can satisfy the claims of the divine law" (*Sons and Daughters of God,* p. 57).

*To withstand the allurements*—"Those who will put on the whole armor of God and devote some time every day in meditation and prayer and to the study of the Scriptures will be connected with heaven and will have a saving, transforming influence upon those around them. Great thoughts, noble aspirations, clear perceptions of truth and duty to God, will be theirs. They will be yearning for purity, for light, for love, for all the graces of heavenly birth. Their earnest prayers will enter into that within the veil. This class will have a sanctified boldness to come into the presence of the Infinite One. They will feel that heaven's light and glories are for them, and they will become refined, elevated, ennobled by this intimate acquaintance with God. Such is the privilege of true Christians.

"Abstract meditation is not enough; busy action is not enough; both are essential to the formation of Christian character. Strength acquired in earnest, secret prayer prepares us to withstand the allurements of society" (*Testimonies for the Church,* vol. 5, pp. 112, 113).

*Secret prayer first*—"We must receive light and blessing, that we may have something to impart. It is the privilege of every worker first to talk with God in the secret place of prayer and then to talk with the people as God's mouthpiece. Men and women who commune with God, who have an abiding Christ, make the very atmosphere holy, because they are cooperating with holy angels. Such witness is needed for this time. We need the melting power of God, the power to draw with Christ" (*Testimonies for the Church*, vol. 6, p. 52).

*Not plead in vain*—"Those who seek God in secret telling the Lord their needs and pleading for help, will not plead in vain. 'Thy Father which seeth in secret Himself shall reward thee openly.' As we make Christ our daily companion we shall feel that the powers of an unseen world are all around us; and by looking unto Jesus we shall become assimilated to His image. By beholding we become changed. The character is softened, refined, and ennobled for the heavenly kingdom. The sure result of our intercourse and fellowship with our Lord will be to increase piety, purity, and fervor. There will be a growing intelligence in prayer. We are receiving a divine education, and this is illustrated in a life of diligence and zeal.

"The soul that turns to God for its help, its support, its power, by daily, earnest prayer, will have noble aspirations, clear perceptions of truth and duty, lofty purposes of action, and a continual hungering and thirsting after righteousness. By maintaining a connection with God, we shall be enabled to diffuse to others, through our association with them, the light, the peace, the serenity, that rules in our hearts. The strength acquired in prayer to God, united with persevering effort in training the mind in thoughtfulness and care-taking, prepares one for daily duties and keeps the spirit in peace under all circumstances.

"If we draw near to God, He will put a word in our mouth to speak for Him, even praise unto His name. He will teach us a strain from the song of the angels, even thanksgiving to our heavenly Father. In every act of life, the light and love of an indwelling Saviour will be revealed. Outward troubles cannot reach the life that is lived by faith in the Son of God" (*Thoughts from the Mount of Blessing,* pp. 85, 86).

*Preparation for missionary work*—"There is great need of self-examination and secret prayer. God has promised wisdom to those who ask Him. Missionary labor is frequently entered upon by those unprepared for the work. Outward zeal is cultivated, while secret prayer is neglected. When this is the case, much harm is done" (*Testimonies for the Church,* vol. 3, pp. 115, 116).

*For a clear view*—"The Lord speaks; enter into your closet, and in silence commune with your own heart; listen to the voice of truth and conscience. Nothing will give such clear views of self as secret prayer. He who seeth in secret and knoweth all things will enlighten your understanding and answer your petitions. Plain, simple duties that must not be neglected will open before you. Make a covenant with God to yield yourselves and all your powers to His service" (*Testimonies for the Church,* vol. 5, p. 163).

***Before speaking with men***—"Personal effort for others should be preceded by much secret prayer; for it requires great wisdom to understand the science of saving souls. Before communicating with men, commune with Christ. At the throne of heavenly grace obtain a preparation for ministering to the people.

"Let your heart break for the longing it has for God, for the living God. The life of Christ has shown what humanity can do by being partaker of the divine nature. All that Christ received from God we too may have. Then ask and receive. With the persevering faith of Jacob, with the unyielding persistence of Elijah, claim for yourself all that God has promised.

"Let the glorious conceptions of God possess your mind. Let your life be knit by hidden links to the life of Jesus. He who commanded the light to shine out of darkness is willing to shine in your heart, to give the light of the knowledge of the glory of God in the face of Jesus Christ. The Holy Spirit will take the things of God and show them unto you, conveying them as a living power into the obedient heart. Christ will lead you to the threshold of the Infinite. You may behold the glory beyond the veil, and reveal to men the sufficiency of Him who ever liveth to make intercession for us" (*Christ's Object Lessons*, p. 149).

***Confidential with God***—" 'When thou prayest, enter into thy closet.' Have a place for secret prayer. Jesus had select places for communion with God, and so should we. We need often to retire to some spot, however humble, where we can be alone with God.

" 'Pray to thy Father which is in secret.' In the name of Jesus we may come into God's presence with the confidence of a child. No man is needed to act as a mediator. Through Jesus we may open our hearts to God as to one who knows and loves us.

"In the secret place of prayer, where no eye but God's can see, no ear but His can hear, we may pour out our most hidden desires and longings to the Father of infinite pity, and in the hush and silence of the soul that voice which never fails to answer the cry of human need will speak to our hearts.

" 'The Lord is very pitiful, and of tender mercy.' James 5:11. He waits with unwearied love to hear the confessions of the wayward and to accept their penitence. He watches for some return of gratitude from us, as the mother watches for the smile of recognition from her beloved child. He would have us understand how earnestly and tenderly His heart yearns over us. He invites us to take our trials to His sympathy, our sorrows to His love, our wounds to His healing, our weakness to His strength, our emptiness to His fullness. Never has one been disappointed who came unto Him. 'They looked unto Him, and were lightened: and their faces were not ashamed.' Psalm 34: 5" (*Thoughts from the Mount of Blessing,* pp. 84, 85).

***Christ sees us***—"While they trust to the guidance of human authority, none will come to a saving knowledge of the truth. Like Nathanael, we need to study God's word for ourselves, and pray for the enlightenment of the Holy Spirit. He who saw Nathanael under the fig tree will see us in the secret place of prayer. Angels from the world of light are near to those who in humility seek for divine guidance" (*The Desire of Ages*, p. 141).

***Secret prayer – everywhere***—"It is a wonderful thing that we can pray effectually; that unworthy, erring mortals possess the power of offering their requests to God. What higher power can man desire than this, to be linked with the infinite God? Feeble, sinful man has the privilege of speaking to his Maker. We may utter words that reach the throne of the Monarch of the universe. We may speak with Jesus as we walk by the way, and He says, I am at thy right hand.

"We may commune with God in our hearts; we may walk in companionship with Christ. When engaged in our daily labor, we may breathe out our heart's desire, inaudible to any human ear; but that word cannot die away into silence, nor can it be lost. Nothing can drown the soul's desire. It rises above the din of the street, above the noise of machinery. It is God to whom we are speaking, and our prayer is heard. Ask, then; ask, and ye shall receive. Ask for humility, wisdom, courage, increase of faith. To every sincere prayer an answer will come. It may not come just as you desire, or at the time you look for it; but it will come in the way and at the time that will best meet your need. The prayers you offer in loneliness, in weariness, in trial, God answers, not always according to your expectations, but always for your good" (*Gospel Workers,* p. 258).

- *Chapter Twenty-nine* -

# *Praying Through*

***Pray always***—"Without unceasing prayer and diligent watching we are in danger of growing careless and of deviating from the right path. The adversary seeks continually to obstruct the way to the mercy seat" (*Steps to Christ,* p. 95).

***Let nothing hinder you***—"Let nothing, however dear, however loved, absorb your mind and affections, diverting you from the study of God's Word or from earnest prayer" (*Testimonies for the Church*, vol. 8, p. 53).

"Holiness is not rapture: it is an entire surrender of the will to God; it is living by

65

every word that proceeds from the mouth of God; it is doing the will of our heavenly Father" (*The Acts of the Apostles,* p. 51).

***Stronger confidence***—"Stronger and stronger should be our confidence that God's Spirit will be with us, making us pure and holy, as upright and fragrant as the cedar of Lebanon" (*Gospel Workers,* p. 272).

"That prayer which comes forth from an earnest believing heart is the effectual, fervent prayer that availeth much. God does not always answer our prayers as we expect, for we may not ask what would be for our highest good; but in His infinite love and wisdom He will give us those things which we most need" (*Testimonies for the Church,* vol. 4, p. 531).

***Fills with divine love***—"What God promises, He is able at any time to perform, and the work which He gives His people to do, He is able to accomplish by them" (*Counsels on Health,* p. 378).

"It is better for us that God does not always answer our prayers just when we desire, and in just the manner we wish" (*Counsels on Health,* p. 378).

"Our petitions must not take the form of a command, but of intercession for Him to do the things we desire of Him" (*Counsels on Health,* p. 379).

***Fills with divine love***—"On the Day of Pentecost the Infinite One revealed Himself in power to the church....

"The hearts of the disciples were surcharged with a benevolence so full, so deep, so far-reaching, that it impelled them to go to the ends of the earth testifying: God forbid that we should glory, save in the cross of our Lord Jesus Christ" (*Testimonies for the Church,* vol. 7, p. 31).

"By earnest, persevering prayer they obtained the endowment of the Holy Spirit, and then they went forth, weighted with the burden of saving souls, filled with zeal to extend the triumphs of the cross" (*Testimonies for the Church,* vol. 7, p. 32).

"Is not the Spirit of God to come today in answer to earnest, persevering prayer, and fill men with power?" (*Testimonies for the Church,* vol. 7, p. 32).

"What the Lord did for His people in that time, it is just as essential, and more so, that He do for His people today" (*Testimonies for the Church,* vol. 7, p. 33).

*- Chapter Thirty -*

# Silent Prayer Everywhere

***Even the silent petition***—"The Lord will accept even the silent petition of the burdened heart" (*S.D.A. Bible Commentary*, vol. 2, p. 1014; The Youth's Instructor, Nov. 17, 1898).

***Appropriate everywhere***—"There is no time or place in which it is inappropriate to offer up a petition to God. There is nothing that can prevent us from lifting up our hearts in the spirit of earnest prayer. In the crowds of the street, in the midst of a business engagement, we may send up a petition to God and plead for divine guidance, as did Nehemiah when he made his request before King Artaxerxes. A closet of communion may be found wherever we are. We should have the door of the heart open continually and our invitation going up that Jesus may come and abide as a heavenly guest in the soul" (*Steps to Christ,* p. 99).

***Walking by the way***—"Let all who are afflicted or unjustly used, cry to God. Turn away from those whose hearts are as steel, and make your requests known to your Maker. Never is one repulsed who comes to Him with a contrite heart. Not one sincere prayer is lost. Amid the anthems of the celestial choir, God hears the cries of the weakest human being. We pour out our heart's desire in our closets, we breathe a prayer as we walk by the way, and our words reach the Monarch of the universe. They may be inaudible to any human ear, but they cannot die away into silence, nor can they be lost through the activities of business that are going on. Nothing can drown the soul's desire. It rises above the din of the street, above the confusion of the multitude, to the heavenly courts. It is God to whom we are speaking, and our prayer is heard" (*Christ's Object Lessons*, p. 174).

***Every breath***—"Cultivate the habit of talking with the Saviour when you are alone, when you are walking, and when you are busy with your daily labor. Let the heart be continually uplifted in silent petition for help, for light, for strength, for knowledge. Let every breath be a prayer" (*The Ministry of Healing*, pp. 510, 511).

***The way to the throne***—"The way to the throne of God is always open. You cannot always be on your knees in prayer, but your silent petitions may constantly ascend to God for strength and guidance. When tempted, as you will be, you may flee to the secret place of the Most High. His everlasting arms will be underneath you" (*Counsels on Health*, p. 362).

*Combine with earnest work*—"We must live a twofold life a life of thought and action, of silent prayer and earnest work. The strength received through communion with God, united with earnest effort in training the mind to thoughtfulness and caretaking, prepares one for daily duties and keeps the spirit in peace under all circumstances, however trying" (*The Ministry of Healing,* p. 512).

*While hands are employed*—"If the rush of work is allowed to drive us from our purpose of seeking the Lord daily, we shall make the greatest mistakes; we shall incur losses, for the Lord is not with us; we have closed the door so that He cannot find access to our souls. But if we pray even when our hands are employed, the Saviour's ear is open to hear our petitions. If we are determined not to be separated from the Source of our strength, Jesus will be just as determined to be at our right hand to help us, that we may not be put to shame before our enemies. The grace of Christ can accomplish for us that which all our efforts will fail to do. Those who love and fear God may be surrounded with a multitude of cares, and yet not falter or make crooked paths for their feet. God takes care of you in the place where it is your duty to be" (*Counsels on Health,* p. 424).

- Chapter Thirty-one -

# Prayer and Meditation

*Meditate upon His love*—"God bids us fill the mind with great thoughts, pure thoughts. He desires us to meditate upon His love and mercy, to study His wonderful work in the great plan of redemption. Then clearer and still clearer will be our perception of truth, higher, holier, our desire for purity of heart and clearness of thought. The soul dwelling in the pure atmosphere of holy thought will be transformed by communion with God through the study of the Scriptures" (*Christ's Object Lessons,* p. 60).

*With Bible study*—"The Bible should never be studied without prayer. The Holy Spirit alone can cause us to feel the importance of those things easy to be understood, or prevent us from wresting truths difficult of comprehension. It is the office of heavenly angels to…prepare the heart so to comprehend God's Word that we shall be charmed with its beauty, admonished by its warnings, or animated and strengthened by its promises" (*The Great Controversy,* pp. 599, 600).

*Claim and obey*—"A true knowledge of the Bible can be gained only through the aid of that Spirit by whom the Word was given. And in order to gain this knowledge we must live by it. All that God's Word commands, we are to obey. ALL that it promises, we may claim" (*Education*, p. 189).

**Singleness of purpose**—"An understanding of the Bible truth depends not so much on the power of intellect brought to the search as on the singleness of purpose, the earnest longing after righteousness" (*The Great Controversy*, p. 599).

**Walk in the light**—"Walk continually in the light of God. Meditate day and night upon His character. Then you will see His beauty and rejoice in His goodness. Your heart will glow with a sense of His love. You will be uplifted as if borne by everlasting arms. With the power and light that God imparts, you can comprehend more and accomplish more than you ever before deemed possible" (*The Ministry of Healing*, p. 514).

**Meditate on the perfection of the Saviour**—"As we meditate upon the perfection of the Saviour, we shall desire to be wholly transformed, and renewed in the image of His purity. There will be a hungering and thirsting of soul to become like Him whom we adore. The more our thoughts are upon Christ, the more we shall speak of Him to others and represent Him to the world" (*Steps to Christ*, p. 89).

**Living at the end**—"We are living in the most solemn period of this world's history.…We need to humble ourselves before the Lord, with fasting and prayer, and to meditate much upon His Word, especially upon the scenes of the judgment. We should now seek a deep and living experience in the things of God. We have not a moment to lose. Events of vital importance are taking place around us; we are on Satan's enchanted ground" (*The Great Controversy*, p. 601).

- Chapter Thirty-two -

# Angels and Prayer

**Hovering near**—"As the praying ones continued their earnest cries, at times a ray of light from Jesus came to them, to encourage their hearts and light up their countenances. Some, I saw, did not participate in this work of agonizing and pleading. They seemed indifferent and careless. They were not resisting the darkness around them, and it shut them in like a thick cloud. The angels of God left these and went to the aid of the earnest, praying ones. I saw angels of God hasten to the assistance of all who were struggling with all their power to resist the evil angels and trying to help themselves by calling upon God with perseverance. But His angels left those who made no effort to help themselves, and I lost sight of them" (*Early Writings*, p. 270).

*Teaching how to pray*—"Church members, young and old, should be educated to go forth to proclaim this last message to the world. If they go in humility, angels of God will go with them, teaching them how to lift up the voice in prayer, how to raise the voice in song, and how to proclaim the gospel message for this time" (*My Life Today,* p. 238).

*Minister to the sick*—"Often in the care of the suffering, much attention is given to minor matters, while the patients' need of the great all-saving truths of the gospel, which would minister to both soul and body, is forgotten. When you neglect to offer prayer for the sick, you deprive them of great blessings; for angels of God are waiting to minister to these souls in response to your petitions" (*Medical Ministry*, p. 195).

*Listening to your prayers*—"Could men see with heavenly vision, they would behold companies of angels that excel in strength stationed about those who have kept the word of Christ's patience. With sympathizing tenderness, angels have witnessed their distress and have heard their prayers" (*The Great Controversy,* p. 630).

*Writing and recording them*—"The recording angels write the history of the holy struggles and conflicts of the people of God;…[and] record their prayers and tears" (*The Acts of the Apostles,* p. 561).

*Present prayers to God*—"Those who look unto Jesus day by day and hour by hour, who watch unto prayer, are drawing nigh to Jesus. Angels with wings out-spread wait to bear their contrite prayers to God, and to register them in the books of heaven" (*S.D.A. Bible Commentary*, vol. 4, p. 1184; Letter 90, 1895).

*Appointed to answer*—"Heavenly beings are appointed to answer the prayers of those who are working unselfishly for the interests of the cause of God. The very highest angels in the heavenly courts are appointed to work out the prayers which ascend to God for the advancement of the cause of God. Each angel has his particular post of duty, which he is not permitted to leave for any other place" (*S.D.A. Bible Commentary*, vol. 4, p. 1173; Letter 201, 1899).

**Sent to answer**—"Ministering angels are waiting about the throne to instantly obey the mandate of Jesus Christ to answer every prayer offered in earnest, living faith" (*Selected Messages,* book 2, p. 377).

**Come to our help**—"We may through the exercise of faith and prayer, call to our side a retinue of heavenly angels, who will guard us from every corrupting influence" (*Our High Calling*, p. 23).

**Bring many blessings**—"Angels are constantly bringing blessing and hope, courage and help, to the children of men" (*The Acts of the Apostles,* p. 153).

"Strength and grace have been provided through Christ to be brought by ministering angels to every believing soul" (*Steps to Christ,* p. 53).

**Influencing your actions**—"When you rise in the morning, do you feel your helplessness and your need of strength from God?... If so, angels mark your prayers, and if these prayers have not gone forth out of feigned lips, when you are in danger of unconsciously doing wrong and exerting an influence which will lead others to do wrong, your guardian angels will be by your side, prompting you to a better course, choosing your words for you and influencing your actions" (*Testimonies for the Church,* vol. 3, pp. 363, 364).

**Why do we pray so little?**—"What can the angels think of poor helpless human beings, who are subject to temptation, when God's heart of infinite love yearns toward them, ready to give them more than they can ask or think, and yet they pray so little and have so little faith? The angels love to bow before God; they love to be near Him. They regard communion with God as their highest joy; and yet the children of earth, who need so much the help that God only can give, seem satisfied to walk without the light of His Spirit, the companionship of His presence" (*Steps to Christ,* p. 94).

- Chapter Thirty-three -

# Why Pray if God Already Knows?

**We ask because God says, "Ask and ye shall receive"**—"Our prayers are not to inform God of something He does not know. The Lord is acquainted with the secrets of every soul" (*Messages to Young People,* p. 247).

"Even before the prayer is uttered,…grace from Christ goes forth to meet the grace that is working upon the human soul" (*Christ's Object Lessons*, p. 206).

"It is a part of God's plan to grant us, in answer to the prayer of faith, that which He would not bestow did we not thus ask" (*The Great Controversy*, p. 525).

*Continue to ask*—"God has a heaven full of blessings that He wants to bestow on those who are earnestly seeking for that help which the Lord alone can give" (*Sons and Daughters of God*, p. 123).

"When you have asked for things that are necessary for your soul's good, believe that you receive them, and you shall have them" (*My Life Today*, p. 16).

*Continue to ask*—"God does not say, Ask once and you shall receive. He bids us ask. Unwearyingly persist in prayer. The persistent asking brings the petitioner into a more earnest attitude, and gives him an increased desire to receive the things for which he asks" (*Christ's Object Lessons*, p. 145).

"You need to watch, lest the busy activities of life lead you to neglect prayer when you most need the strength prayer would give.…It is a great evil to defraud the soul of the strength and heavenly wisdom which are waiting your demand" (*Testimonies for the Church*, vol. 5, p. 560).

"Do just what He [God] has told you to do, and be assured that God will do all that He has said He would do" (*Our High Calling*, p. 97).

"The sense of our need leads us to pray earnestly, and our heavenly Father is moved by our supplications" (*Christ's Object Lessons*, p. 172).

"It is only as we ask in earnest prayer, that God will grant us our heart's desire" (*Gospel Workers*, p. 255).

*Quest for power through prayer*—"The greatest victories gained for the cause of God are not the result of labored argument;…they are gained in the audience chamber with God" (*Gospel Workers*, p. 259).

- Chapter Thirty-four -

# God Hears Your Prayers

*He hears and answers*—"And God hears prayer. Christ has said, 'If ye shall ask anything in My name, I will do it.' Again He says, 'If any man serve Me, him will My Father honor.' John 14:14; 12:26. If we live according to His word, every precious promise He has given will be fulfilled to us. We are undeserving of His mercy, but as we give ourselves to Him, He receives us. He will work for and through those who follow Him" (*The Ministry of Healing,* pp. 226, 227).

*He hears, tastes, cares*—"The infinite God, said Jesus, makes it your privilege to approach Him by the name of Father. Understand all that this implies. No earthly parent ever pleaded so earnestly with an erring child as He who made you pleads with the transgressor. No human, loving interest ever followed the impenitent with such tender invitations. God dwells in every abode; He hears every word that is spoken, listens to every prayer that is offered, tastes the sorrows and disappointments of every soul, regards the treatment that is given to father, mother, sister, friend, and neighbor. He cares for our necessities, and His love and mercy and grace are continually flowing to satisfy our need.

"But if you call God your Father you acknowledge yourselves His children, to be guided by His wisdom and to be obedient in all things, knowing that His love is changeless. You will accept His plan for your life" (*Thoughts from the Mount of Blessing,* p. 105).

*Hear and answer*—"The Lord will certainly hear and answer the prayers of His workers if they will seek Him for counsel and instruction" (*Evangelism,* p. 399).

*Caring for the needy*—"It is the Lord's purpose that His method of healing without drugs shall be brought into prominence in every large city through our medical institutions. God invests with holy dignity those who go forth farther and still farther, in every place to which it is possible to obtain entrance. Satan will make the work as difficult as possible, but divine power will attend all truehearted workers. Guided by our heavenly Father's hand, let us go forward, improving every opportunity to extend the work of God.

"The Lord speaks to all medical missionaries, saying: Go, work today in My vineyard to save souls. God hears the prayers of all who seek Him in truth. He has the power that we all need. He fills the heart with love, and joy, and peace, and holiness. Character is constantly being developed. We cannot afford to spend the time working at cross-purposes with God" (*Testimonies for the Church*, vol. 9, p. 169).

*When praying for conversions*—"When those who know the truth practice the self-denial enjoined in God's word, the message will go with power. The Lord will hear our prayers for the conversion of souls. God's people will let their light shine forth, and unbelievers, seeing their good works, will glorify our heavenly Father" (*Messages to Young People*, p. 315).

***Our part and His***—"Your feeling of dependence will drive you to prayer, and your sense of duty summons you to effort. Prayer and effort, effort and prayer, will be the business of your life. You must pray as though the efficiency and praise were all due to God, and labor as though duty were all your own. If you want power you may have it; it is waiting your draft upon it. Only believe in God, take Him at His word, act by faith, and blessings will come.

"In this matter, genius, logic, and eloquence will not avail. Those who have a humble, trusting, contrite heart, God accepts, and hears their prayer; and when God helps, all obstacles will be overcome" (*Testimonies for the Church*, vol. 4, pp. 538, 539).

- Chapter Thirty-five -

# Depend Not on Feelings

***Feelings not a safe test***—"Many make a serious mistake in their religious life by keeping the attention fixed upon their feelings and thus judging of their advancement or decline. Feelings are not a safe criterion. We are not to look within for evidence of our acceptance with God. We shall find there nothing but that which will discourage us. Our only hope is in 'looking unto Jesus the Author and Finisher of our faith'" (*Testimonies for the Church*, vol. 5, pp. 199, 200).

***Principle more important than feeling***—"Feelings are often deceiving, emotions are no sure safeguard; for they are variable and subject to external circumstances. Many are deluded by relying on sensational impressions. The test is: What are you doing for Christ? What sacrifices are you making? What victories are you gaining? A selfish spirit overcome, a temptation to neglect duty resisted, passion subdued, and willing, cheerful obedience rendered to the will of Christ are far greater evidences that you are a child of God than spasmodic piety and emotional religion" (*Testimonies for the Church*, vol. 4, p. 188).

***Principle more important than feeling***—"I saw that the Christian should not set too high a value, or depend too much, upon a happy flight of feeling. These feelings are not always true guides. It should be the study of every Christian to serve God from principle, and not be ruled by feeling. By so doing, faith will be brought into exercise, and will increase. I was shown that if the Christian lives a humble, self-sacrificing life, peace and joy in the Lord will result. But the greatest happiness experienced will be in doing others good, in making others happy. Such happiness will be lasting" (*Testimonies for the Church*, vol. 1, p. 161).

*Feelings can be deceiving*—"Satan leads people to think that because they have felt a rapture of feeling they are converted. But their experience does not change. Their actions are the same as before. Their lives show no good fruit. They pray often and long, and are constantly referring to the feelings they had at such and such a time. But they do not live the new life. They are deceived. Their experience goes no deeper than feeling. They build upon the sand, and when adverse winds come their house is swept away.…

"They overlook the fact that the believer in Christ must work out his own salvation with fear and trembling. The convicted sinner has something to do. He must repent and show true faith.…

"What is the sign of a new heart? A changed life. There is a daily, hourly dying to selfishness and pride" (*Messages to Young People*, pp. 71, 72).

*- Chapter Thirty-six -*

# When and How Will God Answer Prayer?

*Answers will come*—"God has sent us to work in His vineyard. It is our business to do all we can. 'In the morning sow thy seed, and in the evening withhold not thine hand: for thou knowest not whether shall prosper, either this or that.' We have too little faith. We limit the Holy One of Israel. We should be grateful that God condescends to use any of us as His instruments. For every earnest prayer put up in faith for anything, answers will be returned. They may not come just as we have expected; but they will come, not perhaps as we have devised, but at the very time when we most need them. But, oh, how sinful is our unbelief! 'If ye abide in Me, and My words abide in you, ye shall ask what ye will, and it shall be done unto you'" (*Testimonies for the Church*, vol. 3, p. 209).

*May not come quickly*—"Christ's two days' delay after hearing that Lazarus was sick was not a neglect or a denial on His part.…This should be an encouragement to us.…We are to rest in the Lord, and wait patiently for Him. The answer to our prayers may not come as quickly as we desire, and it may not be just what we have asked; but He who knows what is for the highest good of His children will bestow a much greater good than we have asked, if we do not become faithless and discouraged" (*Sons and Daughters of God,* p. 92).

***When and how***—"I saw that the servants of God and the church were too easily discouraged. When they asked their Father in heaven for things which they thought they needed, and these did not immediately come, their faith wavered, their courage fled, and a murmuring feeling took possession of them. This, I saw, displeased God.

"Every saint who comes to God with a true heart, and sends his honest petitions to Him in faith, will have his prayers answered. Your faith must not let go of the promises of God, if you do not see or feel the immediate answer to your prayers. Be not afraid to trust God. Rely upon His sure promise: 'Ask, and ye shall receive.' God is too wise to err, and too good to withhold any good thing from his saints that walk uprightly. Man is erring, and although his petitions are sent up from an honest heart, he does not always ask for the things that are good for himself, or that will glorify God. When this is so, our wise and good Father hears our prayers, and will answer, sometimes immediately; but He gives us the things that are for our best good and His own glory. God gives us blessings; if we could look into His plan, we would clearly see that He knows what is best for us and that our prayers are answered. Nothing hurtful is given, but the blessing we need, in the place of something we asked for that would not be good for us, but to our hurt.

"I saw that if we do not feel immediate answers to our prayers, we should hold fast our faith, not allowing distrust to come in, for that will separate us from God. If our faith wavers, we shall receive nothing from Him. Our confidence in God should be strong; and when we need it most, the blessing will fall upon us like a shower of rain.

"When the servants of God pray for His Spirit and blessing, it sometimes comes immediately; but it is not always then bestowed. At such times, faint not. Let your faith hold fast the promise that it will come. Let your trust be fully in God, and often that blessing will come when you need it most, and you will unexpectedly receive help from God when you are presenting the truth to unbelievers, and will be enabled to speak the word with clearness and power.

"It was represented to me like children asking a blessing of their earthly parents who love them. They ask something that the parent knows will hurt them; the parent gives them the things that will be good and healthful for them, in place of that which they desired. I saw that every prayer which is sent up in faith from an honest heart will be heard of God and answered, and the one that sent up the petition will have the blessing when he needs it most, and it will often exceed his expectations. Not a prayer of a true saint is lost if sent up in faith from an honest heart" (*Testimonies for the Church,* vol. 1, pp. 120, 121).

***Come when and how needed***—"Ask, then; ask, and ye shall receive. Ask for humility, wisdom, courage, increase of faith. To every sincere prayer an answer will come. It may not come just as you desire, or at the time you look for it; but it will come in the way and at the time that will best meet your need. The prayers you offer in loneliness, in weariness, in trial, God answers, not always according to your expectations, but always for your good" (*Gospel Workers,* p. 258).

***In faith, keep working and praying***—"The lessons that God sends will always, if well learned, bring help in due time. Put your trust in God. Pray much, and believe. Trusting, hoping, believing, holding fast the hand of Infinite Power, you will be more than conquerors.

"True workers walk and work by faith. Sometimes they grow weary with watching the slow advance of the work when the battle wages strong between the powers of good and evil. But if they refuse to fail or be discouraged they will see the clouds breaking away and the promise of deliverance fulfilling. Through the mist with which Satan has surrounded them, they will see the shining of the bright beams of the Sun of Righteousness.

"Work in faith, and leave results with God. Pray in faith, and the mystery of His providence will bring its answer. At times it may seem that you cannot succeed. But work and believe, putting into your efforts faith, hope, and courage. After doing what you can, wait for the Lord, declaring His faithfulness, and He will bring His word to pass. Wait, not in fretful anxiety, but in undaunted faith and unshaken trust" (*Testimonies for the Church,* vol. 7, p. 245; read the entire chapter).

***In best way at best time***—"Another element of prevailing prayer is faith. 'He that cometh to God must believe that He is, and that He is a rewarder of them that diligently seek Him.' Hebrews 11:6. Jesus said to His disciples, 'What things soever ye desire, when ye pray, believe that ye receive them.' Mark 11:24. Do we take Him at His word?

"The assurance is broad and unlimited, and He is faithful who has promised. When we do not receive the very things we asked for, at the time we ask, we are still to believe that the Lord hears and that He will answer our prayers. We are so erring and shortsighted that we sometimes ask for things that would not be a blessing to us, and our heavenly Father in love answers our prayers by giving us that which will be for our highest good that which we ourselves would desire if with vision divinely enlightened we could see all things as they really are. When our prayers seem not to be answered, we are to cling to the promise; for the time of answering will surely come, and we shall receive the blessing we need most. But to claim that prayer will always be answered in the very way and for the particular thing that we desire, is presumption. God is too wise to err, and too good to withhold any good thing from them that walk uprightly. Then do not fear to trust Him, even though you do not see the immediate answer to your prayers. Rely upon His sure promise, 'Ask, and it shall be given you'" (*Steps to Christ,* p. 96).

***Not always according to expectation***—"While you prayed in your affliction for peace in Christ, a cloud of darkness seemed to blacken across your mind. The rest and peace did not come as your expected. At times your faith seemed to be tested to the utmost. As you looked back to your past life, you saw sorrow and disappointment; as you viewed the future, all was uncertainty. The divine Hand led you wondrously to bring you to the cross and to teach you that God was indeed a rewarder of those who diligently seek Him. Those who ask aright will receive. He that seeketh in faith shall find. The experience gained in the furnace of trial and affliction is worth more than all the inconvenience and painful experience it costs" (*Testimonies for the Church*, vol. 3, p. 415).

*Forgiveness of sin – immediately*—"In some instances of healing, Jesus did not at once grant the blessing sought. But in the case of leprosy no sooner was the appeal made than it was granted. When we pray for earthly blessings, the answer to our prayer may be delayed, or God may give us something other than we ask; but not so when we ask for deliverance from sin. It is His will to cleanse us from sin, to make us His children, and to enable us to live a holy life" (*The Ministry of Healing*, p. 70).

*Delays test faith and sincerity*—"There are precious promises in the Scriptures to those who wait upon the Lord. We all desire an immediate answer to our prayers and are tempted to become discouraged if our prayer is not immediately answered.... The delay is for our special benefit. We have a chance to see whether our faith is true and sincere or changeable like the waves of the sea. We must bind ourselves upon the altar with the strong cords of faith and love, and let patience have her perfect work" (*Counsels on Health*, pp. 380, 381).

*Delays give opportunity for heart searching*—"God does not always answer our prayers the first time we call upon Him; for should He do this, we might take it for granted that we had a right to all the blessings and favors He bestowed upon us. Instead of searching our hearts to see if any evil was entertained by us, any sin indulged, we should become careless, and fail to realize our dependence upon Him, and our need of His help" (*S.D.A. Bible Commentary*, vol. 2, p. 1035; *The Review and Herald*, Mar. 27, 1913).

*God does not forget*—"Throughout his married life, Zacharias had prayed for a son. He and his wife were now old, and as yet their prayer had remained unanswered; but he murmured not. God had not forgotten. He had His appointed time for answering his prayer, and when the case seemed hopeless, Zacharias received his answer....God had not forgotten the prayer of His servants. He had written it in His record book, to be answered in His own good time" (*S.D.A. Bible Commentary*, vol. 5, p. 1114; Ms 27, 1898).

- *Chapter Thirty-seven* -

# *Will the Answers Come?*

***He can and will***—"There is strength to be obtained of God. He can help. He can give grace and heavenly wisdom. If you ask in faith, you will receive; but you must watch unto prayer. Watch, pray, work, should be your watchword" (*Testimonies for the Church*, vol. 2, p. 427).

***Answers to petition and thanksgiving***—"Let us waste no time in deploring the scantiness of our visible resources, but let us make the best use of what we have. Though the outward appearance may be unpromising, energy and trust in God will develop resources. Let us send in our offerings with thanksgiving and with prayer that the Lord will bless the gifts and multiply them as He did the food given to the five thousand. If we use the very best facilities we have, the power of God will enable us to reach the multitudes that are starving for the bread of life.

"Faith is the spiritual hand that touches infinity.

"Workers for Christ are never to think, much less to speak, of failure in their work. The Lord Jesus is our efficiency in all things; His Spirit is to be our inspiration; and as we place ourselves in His hands, to be channels of light, our means of doing good will never be exhausted. We may draw upon His fullness and receive of that grace which has no limit" (*Testimonies for the Church*, vol. 6, p. 467).

***If answers are not immediate***—"After the prayer is made, if the answer is not realized immediately, do not weary of waiting and become unstable. Waver not. Cling to the promise, 'Faithful is He that calleth you, who also will do it.' Like the importunate widow, urge your case, being firm in your purpose. Is the object important and of great consequence to you? It certainly is. Then waver not, for your faith may be tried. If the thing you desire is valuable, it is worthy of a strong, earnest effort. You have the promise; watch and pray. Be steadfast and the prayer will be answered; for is it not God who has promised? If it costs you something to obtain it you will prize it the more when obtained. You are plainly told that if you waver you need not think that you shall receive anything of the Lord. A caution is here given not to become weary, but to rest firmly upon the promise. If you ask, He will give you liberally and upbraid not" (*Testimonies for the Church*, vol. 2, p. 131).

***Too wise***—"We all desire immediate and direct answers to our prayers, and are tempted to become discouraged when the answer is delayed or comes in an unlooked-for form. But God is too wise and good to answer our prayers always at just the time and in just the manner we desire. He will do more and better for us than to accomplish all our wishes. And because we can trust His wisdom and love, we should not ask Him to concede to our will, but should seek to enter into and accomplish His purpose. Our desires and interests should be lost in His will. These experiences that test faith is true and sincere, resting on the word of God alone, or whether depending on circumstances, it is uncertain and changeable. Faith is strengthened by exercise. We must let patience have its perfect work, remembering that there are precious promises in the Scriptures for those who wait upon the Lord" (*The Ministry of Healing,* pp. 230, 231).

***Helping Him help us***—"In the Word of God are represented two contending parties that influence and control human agencies in our world. Constantly these parties are working with every human being. Those who are under God's control and who are influenced by the heavenly angels, will be able to discern the crafty workings of the unseen powers of darkness. Those who desire to be in harmony with the heavenly agencies should be intensely in earnest to do God's will. They must give no place whatever to Satan and his angels.

"But unless we are constantly on guard, we shall be overcome by the enemy. Although a solemn revelation of God's will concerning us has been revealed to all, yet a knowledge of His will does not set aside the necessity of offering earnest supplications to Him for help, and of diligently seeking to cooperate with Him in answering the prayers offered. He accomplishes His purposes through human instrumentalities" (*S.D.A. Bible Commentary*, vol. 6, p. 1119).

***Lay open everything***—"Every earnest petition for grace and strength will be answered....Ask God to do for you those things that you cannot do for yourselves. Tell Jesus everything. Lay open before Him the secrets of your heart; for His eye searches the inmost recesses of the soul, and He reads your thoughts as an open book. When you have asked for the things that are necessary for your soul's good, believe that you receive them, and you shall have them. Accept His gifts with your whole heart; for Jesus has died that you might have the precious things of heaven as your own, and at last find a home with the heavenly angels in the kingdom of God" (*My Life Today,* p. 16).

***Conditions for successful prayer***—(Read *Steps to Christ*, chapter 11, pages 93-104.)

***He knows what is best - and will give it***—"He who blessed the nobleman at Capernaum is just as desirous of blessing us. But like the afflicted father, we are often led to seek Jesus by the desire for some earthly good; and upon the granting of our request we rest our confidence in His love. The Saviour longs to give us a greater blessing than we ask; and He delays the answer to our request that He may show us us the evil of our own hearts, and our deep need of His grace. He desires us to renounce the selfishness that leads us to seek Him. Confessing our helplessness and bitter need, we are to trust ourselves wholly to His love.

"The nobleman wanted to see the fulfillment of his prayer before he should believe; but he had to accept the word of Jesus that his request was heard and the blessing granted. This lesson we also have to learn. Not because we see or feel that God hears us are we to believe. We are to trust in His promises. When we come to Him in faith, every petition enters the heart of God. When we have asked for His blessing, we should believe that we receive it, and thank Him that we have received it. Then we are to go about our duties, assured that the blessing will be realized when we need it most. When we have learned to do this, we shall know that our prayers are answered. God will do for us 'exceeding abundantly,' 'according to the riches of His glory,' and 'the working of His mighty power.' Ephesians 3:20, 16; 1:19 (*The Desire of Ages,* p. 200).

***Victory through Christ***—"When we seek to gain heaven through the merits of Christ, the soul makes progress. Looking unto Jesus, the Author and Finisher of our faith, we may go on from strength to strength, from victory to victory; for through Christ the grace of God has worked out our complete salvation" (*Selected Messages,* book 1, p. 364).

***In direction for action***—"Jesus does not call on us to follow Him, and then forsake us. If we surrender our lives to His service, we can never be placed in a position for which God has not made provision. Whatever may be our situation, we have a guide to direct our way....

"'All things, whatsoever ye shall ask in prayer, believing, ye shall receive'" (*Gospel Workers,* p. 263).

***Quieting anxiety***—"Summon all your powers to look up, not down at your difficulties; then you will never faint by the way. You will soon see Jesus behind the cloud, reaching out His hand to help you; and all you have to do is to give Him your hand in simple faith and let Him lead you" (*Testimonies for the Church,* vol. 5, p. 578).

***Assurance of sin forgiven***—"It is God's glory to encircle sinful, repentant human beings in the arms of His love, to bind up their wounds, to cleanse them from sin, and to clothe them with the garments of salvation" (*Prophets and Kings,* p. 668).

***A sense of divine companionship***—"Jesus, the Majesty of heaven, proposes to elevate to companionship with Himself those who come to Him with their burdens, their weaknesses, and their cares....

"It is our privilege to have daily a calm, close, happy walk with Jesus" (*Our High Calling*, p. 97).

*A sense of divine companionship*—"Pray in faith, and the mystery of His providence will bring its answer" (*Testimonies for the Church*, vol. 7, p. 245).

*Christ presents our prayers as His own request*—"No sooner does the child of God approach the mercy seat than he becomes the client of the great Advocate. At his first utterance of penitence and appeal for pardon Christ espouses his case and makes it His own, presenting the supplication before the Father as His own request" (*Testimonies for the Church*, vol. 6, p. 364).

- *Chapter Thirty-eight* -

# Obedience and Faith a Condition of Prayer

*Must feel our need*—"There are certain conditions upon which we may expect that God will hear and answer our prayers. One of the first of these is that we feel our need of help from Him" (*Steps to Christ*, p. 95).

*Wholehearted consecration required*—"All who consecrate soul, body, and spirit to God will be constantly receiving a new endowment of physical and mental power. The inexhaustible supplies of heaven are at their command.... Through cooperation with Christ they are complete in Him, and in their human weakness they are enabled to do the deeds of Omnipotence" (*The Desire of Ages*, p. 827).

*Obedience necessary*—"Prayer can never take the place of duty....Those who bring their petitions to God, claiming His promise while they do not comply with the conditions, insult Jehovah. They bring the name of Christ as their authority for the fulfillment of the promise, but they do not those things that would show faith in Christ and love for Him" (*Christ's Object Lessons*, p. 143).

"As the giver of every blessing, God claims a certain portion of all we possess.... But if we withhold from Him that which is His own, how can we claim His blessing? If we are unfaithful stewards of earthly things, how can we expect Him to trust us with the things of heaven? It may be that here is the secret of unanswered prayer" (*Christ's Object Lessons*, p. 144).

"If we render to Him only a partial, halfhearted obedience, His promises will not be fulfilled to us" (*The Ministry of Healing*, p. 227).

*Faith another condition*—"Another element of prevailing prayer is faith....Do we take Him at His word?" (*Steps to Christ,* p. 96).

"We are too faithless. Oh, how I wish that I could lead our people to have faith in God! They need not feel that in order to exercise faith they must be wrought up into a high state of excitement. All they have to do is to believe God's Word, just as they believe one another's word. He hath said it, and He will perform His Word. Calmly rely on His promise, because He means all that He says. Say, He has spoken to me in His Word, and He will fulfill every promise that He has made....Act as if your heavenly Father could be trusted" (*Selected Messages,* book 1, pp. 83, 84).

- Chapter Thirty-nine -

# Confessing and Forgiving

*Receiving God's mercy depends upon us*—"When we come to ask mercy and blessing from God we should have a spirit of love and forgiveness in our own hearts. How can we pray, 'Forgive us our debts, as we forgive our debtors,' and yet indulge an unforgiving spirit? Matthew 6:12. If we expect our own prayers to be heard, we must forgive others in the same manner and to the same extent as we hope to be forgiven" (*Steps to Christ,* p. 97).

*What to do if you have wronged someone*—"If you have given offense to your friend or neighbor, you are to acknowledge your wrong, and it is his duty freely to forgive you. Then you are to seek forgiveness of God, because the brother you have wounded is the property of God, and in injuring him you sinned against his Creator and Redeemer" (*Steps to Christ,* p. 37).

"If we have unwittingly borne false witness, if we have misstated his words, if we have injured his influence in any way, we should go to the ones with whom we have conversed about him, and take back all our injurious misstatements" (*Thoughts from the Mount of Blessing,* p. 59).

"Honesty of intention cannot stand as an excuse for not confessing errors" (*Early Writings,* p. 103).

*True confession is specific*—"True confession is always of a specific character, and acknowledges particular sins. They may be of such a nature as to be brought before God only; they may be wrongs that should be confessed to individuals who have suffered injury through them; or they may be of a public character, and should then be as publicly confessed. But all confession should be definite and to the point, acknowledging the very sins of which you are guilty" (*Steps to Christ,* p. 38).

**Confess before sins are found out**—"There is a vast difference between admitting facts after they have been proved and confessing sins known only to ourselves and to God" (*Patriarchs and Prophets,* p. 498).

"There are those among us who will make confessions, as did Achan, too late to save themselves" (*Testimonies for the Church,* vol. 3, p. 272).

- Chapter Forty -

# Prayer and Healing

**Christ still the Great Physician**—"Our Lord Jesus Christ came to this world as the unwearied servant of man's necessity. He 'took our infirmities, and bare our sicknesses,' that He might minister to every need of humanity" (*The Ministry of Healing,* p. 17).

"He is our refuge in sickness as in health. 'Like as a father pitieth his children, so the Lord pitieth them that fear Him....He sendeth His word, and healeth them, and delivereth them from their destructions.'

"God is just as willing to restore the sick to health now as when the Holy Spirit spoke these words through the psalmist. And Christ is the same compassionate physician now that He was during His earthly ministry. In Him there is healing balm for every disease, restoring power for every infirmity" (*The Ministry of Healing,* pp. 225, 226).

**The source of healing**—"The desire of God for every human being is expressed in the words, 'Beloved, I wish above all things that thou mayest prosper and be in health, even as thy soul prospereth.' 3 John 2.

"He it is who 'forgiveth all thine iniquities; who healeth all thy diseases; who redeemeth thy life from destruction; who crowneth thee with loving-kindness and tender mercies.' Psalm 103:3, 4" (*The Ministry of Healing,* p. 113).

**Cooperation with God necessary**—"The physician should teach his patients that they are to cooperate with God in the work of restoration....He knows that the laws of nature, as truly as the precepts of the Decalogue, are divine, and that only in obedience to them can health be recovered or preserved. He sees many suffering as the result of hurtful practices who might be restored to health if they would do what they might for their own restoration. They need to be taught that every practice which destroys the physical, mental, or spiritual energies is sin, and that health is to be secured through obedience to the laws that God has established for the good of all mankind" (*The Ministry of Healing,* p. 113).

***Use of remedial agencies***—"Those who seek healing by prayer should not neglect to make use of the remedial agencies within their reach. It is not a denial of faith to use such remedies as God has provided to alleviate pain and to aid nature in her work of restoration. It is no denial of faith to cooperate with God, and to place themselves in the condition most favorable to recovery. God has put it in our power to obtain a knowledge of the laws of life. This knowledge has been placed within our reach for use. We should employ every facility for the restoration of health, taking every advantage possible, working in harmony with natural laws" (*The Ministry of Healing,* pp. 231, 232).

***God's purpose in afflictions***—"Many of your afflictions have been visited upon you, in the wisdom of God, to bring you closer to the throne of grace" (*Testimonies for the Church,* vol. 4, p. 143).

***When praying for the sick***—"God knows the end from the beginning. He is acquainted with the hearts of all men. He reads every secret of the soul. He knows whether those for whom prayer is offered would or would not be able to endure the trials that would come upon them should they live. He knows whether their lives would be a blessing or a curse to themselves and to the world. This is one reason why, while presenting our petitions with earnestness, we should say, 'Nevertheless not my will, but Thine, be done.' Luke 22:42. Jesus added these words of submission to the wisdom and will of God when in the Garden of Gethsemane He pleaded, 'O My Father, if it be possible, let this cup pass from Me.' Matthew 26:39. And if they were appropriate for Him, the Son of God, how much more are they becoming on the lips of finite, erring mortals!

"The consistent course is to commit our desires to our all-wise heavenly Father, and then, in perfect confidence, trust all to Him. We know that God hears us if we ask according to His will. But to press our petitions without a submissive spirit is not right; our prayers must take the form, not of command, but of intercession.

"There are cases where God works decidedly by His divine power in the restoration of health. But not all the sick are healed. Many are laid away to sleep in Jesus. John on the Isle of Patmos was bidden write: 'Blessed are the dead which die in the Lord from henceforth: Yea, saith the Spirit, that they may rest from their labors; and their works do follow them.' Revelation 14:13. From this we see that if persons are not raised to health, they should not on this account be judged as wanting in faith" (*The Ministry of Healing,* p. 230).

***An important lesson***—"Not all understand these principles. Many who seek the Lord's healing mercy think that they must have a direct and immediate answer to their prayers or their faith is defective. For this reason, those who are weakened by disease need to he counseled wisely, that they may act with discretion. They should not disregard their duty to the friends who may survive them, or neglect to employ nature's agencies for the restoration of health.

"Often there is danger of error here. Believing that they will be healed in answer to prayer, some fear to do anything that might seem to indicate a lack of faith. But they should not neglect to set their affairs in order as they would desire to do if they expected to be removed by death. Nor should they fear to utter words of encouragement or counsel which at the parting hour they wish to speak to their loved ones" (*The Ministry of Healing,* p. 231).

***Prayer and simple remedies***—"Those who seek healing by prayer should not neglect to make use of the remedial agencies within their reach. It is not a denial of faith to use such remedies as God has provided to alleviate pain and to aid nature in her work of restoration. It is no denial of faith to co-operate with God, and to place themselves in the condition most favorable to recovery. God has put it in our power to obtain a knowledge of the laws of life. This knowledge has been placed within our reach for use. We should employ every facility for the restoration of health, taking every advantage possible, working in harmony with natural laws. When we have prayed for the recovery of the sick, we can work with all the more energy, thanking God that we have the privilege of co-operating with Him, and asking His blessing on the means which He Himself has provided" (*The Ministry of Healing,* pp. 231, 232).

***Prayer for healing a solemn act***—"In the Word of God we have instruction relative to special prayer for the recovery of the sick. But the offering of such prayer is a most solemn act, and should not be entered upon without careful consideration. In many cases of prayer for the healing of the sick, that which is called faith, is nothing less than presumption" (*The Ministry of Healing,* p. 227).

***Beware of fanaticism and false miracle workers***—" 'Why,' asks one and another, 'is not prayer offered for the miraculous healing of the sick, instead of so many sanitariums being established?' Should this be done, great fanaticism would arise in our ranks" (*Evangelism,* p. 594).

" 'Not every one that saith unto Me, Lord, Lord, shall enter into the kingdom of heaven; but he that doeth the will of My Father which is in heaven. Many will say to Me in that day, Lord, Lord, have we not prophesied in Thy name? and in Thy name have cast out devils? and in Thy name done many wonderful works? And then will I profess unto them, I never knew you: depart from Me, ye that work iniquity.' Matthew 7:21-23. These may profess to be followers of Christ, but they have lost sight of their Leader. They may say, 'Lord, Lord;' they may point to the sick who are healed through them, and to other marvelous works, and claim that they have more of the Spirit and power of God than is manifested by those who keep His law. But their works are done under the supervision of the enemy of righteousness, whose aim it is to deceive souls, and are designed to lead away from obedience, truth, and duty. In the near future there will be still more marked manifestations of this miracle-working power" (*S.D.A. Bible Commentary*, vol. 7, pp. 975, 976; *The Signs of the Times,* Feb. 26, 1885).

***Not demand healing, but be submissive to God's will***—"We have united in earnest prayer around the sickbed of men, women, and children, and have felt that they were given back to us from the dead in answer to our earnest prayers. In these prayers we thought we must be positive, and if we exercised faith, that we must ask for nothing less than life. We dared not say, 'If it will glorify God,' fearing it would admit a semblance of doubt. We have anxiously watched those who have been given back, as it were, from the dead. We have seen some of these, especially youth, raised to health, and they have forgotten God, become dissolute in life, causing sorrow and anguish to parents and friends, and have become a shame to those who feared to pray. They lived not to honor and glorify God, but to curse Him with their lives of vice.

"We no longer mark out a way, nor seek to bring the Lord to our wishes. If the life of the sick can glorify Him, we pray that they may live, nevertheless, not as we will but as He will" (*Counsels on Health*, p. 379).

- *Chapter Forty-one* -

# *Prayer In Time of Trouble*

***"As thy days, so shall thy strength be"***—"We are to follow Christ day by day. God does not bestow help for tomorrow. He does not give His children all the directions for their life journey at once, lest they should become confused. He tells them just as much as they can remember and perform. The strength and wisdom imparted are for the present emergency" (*The Desire of Ages,* p. 313).

*Divine comfort*—"Above the distractions of earth He sits enthroned; all things are open to His divine survey; and from His great and calm eternity He orders that which His providence sees best" (*The Ministry of Healing*, p. 417).

"God in His great love is seeking to develop in us the precious graces of His Spirit. He permits us to encounter obstacles, persecution, and hardships, not as a curse, but as the greatest blessing of our lives" (*Thoughts from the Mount of Blessing*, p. 117).

"He measures every trial, He watches the furnace fire that must test every soul" (*Thoughts from the Mount of Blessing*, p. 121).

*"All things work together"*—"The Father's presence encircled Christ, and nothing befell Him but that which infinite love permitted for the blessing of the world. Here was His source of comfort, and it is for us. He who is imbued with the Spirit of Christ abides in Christ. Whatever comes to him comes from the Saviour, who surrounds him with His presence. Nothing can touch him except by the Lord's permission....All experiences and circumstances are God's workmen whereby good is brought to us" (*The Ministry of Healing*, pp. 488, 489).

*Ministry of sorrow*—"In the full light of day, and in the hearing of the music of other voices, the caged bird will not sing the song that his master seeks to teach him. He learns a snatch of this, a trill of that, but never a separate and entire melody. But the master covers the cage, and places it where the bird will listen to the one song he is to sing. In the dark, he tries and tries again to sing that song until it is learned, and he breaks forth in perfect melody. Then the bird is brought forth, and ever after he can sing that song in the light. Thus God deals with His children. He has a song to teach us, and when we have learned it amid the shadows of affliction we can sing it ever afterward" (*The Ministry of Healing*, p. 472).

*Rest in Christ's love*—"Often your mind may be clouded because of pain. Then do not try to think. You know that Jesus loves you. He understands your weakness. You may do His will by simply resting in His arms" (*The Ministry of Healing*, p. 251).

"When temptations assail you, when care, perplexity, and darkness seem to surround your soul, look to the place where you last saw the light. Rest in Christ's love and under His protecting care" (*The Ministry of Healing*, p. 250).

# Chapter Forty-two

# *When the Mind Wanders*

***Bring it back***—"Daily prayer is as essential to growth in grace, and even to spiritual life itself, as is temporal food to physical well-being. We should accustom ourselves to often lift the thoughts to God in prayer. If the mind wanders, we must bring it back; by persevering effort, habit will finally make it easy" (*Messages to Young People*, p. 115).

***Effort required***—"Gird up the loins of your mind, says the apostle; then control your thoughts, not allowing them to have full scope. The thoughts may be guarded and controlled by your own determined efforts" (*The Adventist Home,* p. 54).

***Prayer for help***—"However great one's spiritual light, however much he may enjoy the divine favor and blessing, he should ever walk humbly before the Lord, pleading in faith that God will direct every thought and control every impulse" (*Patriarchs and Prophets*, p. 421).

"Christ alone can direct the thoughts aright" (*Counsels to Parents, Teachers, and Students*, p. 323).

***Be constantly on guard***—"God would have you trust in His love, and be constantly guarding your soul by locking the gate of your thoughts, that they shall not become unmanageable" (*Sons and Daughters of God*, p. 298).

***Listen for God's voice***—"We must individually hear Him speaking to the heart. When every other voice is hushed, and in quietness we wait before Him, the silence of the soul makes more distinct the voice of God. He bids us, 'Be still, and know that I am God.' Psalm 46:10" (*The Desire of Ages,* p. 363).

***Kneel before God***—"Both in public and in private worship it is our privilege to bow on our knees before God when we offer our petitions to Him" (*Prophets and Kings,* p. 48).

"Let this act testify that the whole soul, body, and spirit are in subjection to the Spirit of truth" (*Selected Messages*, book 2, p. 314).

"Man must come on bended knee, as a subject of grace, a suppliant at the footstool of mercy" (*Selected Messages,* book 2, p. 315).

*Praying aloud*—"He [Jesus] spent whole nights in prayer upon the lonely mountains....It was on our account that He poured out His prayers to His Father with strong cries and tears" (*Testimonies for the Church,* vol. 3, p. 379).

"At the sound of fervent prayer, Satan's whole host trembles" (*Testimonies for the Church,* vol. 1, p. 346).

- Chapter Forty-three -

# When Prayer Is Greatly Needed

*The burdened and heavy-laden*—"Invite all who are not satisfied that they are prepared for Christ's coming, and all who feel burdened and heavy-laden, to come apart by themselves. Let those who are spiritual converse with these souls. Pray with and for them. Let much time be spent in prayer and close searching of the word. Let all obtain the real facts of faith in their own souls through belief that the Holy Spirit will be imparted to them because they have a real hungering and thirsting after righteousness. Teach them how to surrender themselves to God, how to believe, how to claim the promises. Let the deep love of God be expressed in words of encouragement, in words of intercession.

"Let there be far more wrestling with God for the salvation of souls. Work disinterestedly, determinedly, with a spirit never to let go. Compel souls to come in to the marriage supper of the Lamb. Let there be more praying, believing, and receiving, and more working together with God" (*Testimonies for the Church,* vol. 6, pp. 65, 66).

*The helpless ones*—"They can pray with and for the helpless ones who have not strength of will to control the appetites that passion has degraded. They can bring a ray of hope into the lives of the defeated and disheartened. Their unselfish love, manifested in acts of disinterested kindness, will make it easier for these suffering ones to believe in the love of Christ" (*The Ministry of Healing,* pp. 144, 145).

*Worldly church members*—"The leaven of godliness has not entirely lost its power. At the time when the danger and depression of the church are greatest, the little company who are standing in the light will be sighing and crying for the abominations that are done in the land. But more especially will their prayers arise in behalf of the church because its members are doing after the manner of the world.

"The earnest prayers of this faithful few will not be in vain. When the Lord comes forth as an avenger, He will also come as a protector of all those who have preserved the faith in its purity and kept themselves unspotted from the world. It is at this time that God has promised to avenge His own elect which cry day and night unto Him, though He bear long with them" (*Testimonies for the Church,* vol. 5, pp. 209, 210; read the entire chapter).

**When men meet in committees**—"When these councils meet, a few words of formal prayer are offered; but the hearts of those present are not brought into harmony with God by earnest, importunate prayer, offered in living faith, in a humble and contrite spirit. If the trustees divorce themselves from the God of wisdom and power, they cannot preserve the high-souled integrity in dealing with their fellow men which God requires. Without divine wisdom, their own spirit will be woven into the decisions they make. If these men are not in communication with God, Satan will surely be one in their councils and will take advantage of their unconsecrated state. Acts of injustice will be done, because God is not presiding. The Spirit of Christ must be an abiding, controlling power over the heart and mind.

"You should take the Lord with you into every one of your councils. If you realize His presence in your assemblies, every action will be conscientiously and prayerfully considered. Every unprincipled motive will be repressed, and uprightness will characterize all your transactions, in small as well as in great matters. Seek counsel of God first, for this is necessary in order that you may counsel together properly" (*Testimonies for the Church,* vol. 5, p. 560).

"God would work mightily for His people today if they would place themselves wholly under His guidance. They need the constant abiding of the Holy Spirit. If there were more prayer in the councils of those bearing responsibilities, more humbling of the heart before God, we should see abundant evidence of divine leadership, and our work would make rapid progress" (*Testimonies for the Church,* vol. 8, p. 238).

**For more time to work**—"A vast responsibility is devolving upon men and women of prayer throughout the land to petition that God will sweep back the cloud of evil and give a few more years of grace in which to work for the Master. Let us cry to God that the angels may hold the four winds until missionaries shall be sent to all parts of the world and shall proclaim the warning against disobeying the law of Jehovah" (*Testimonies for the Church,* vol. 5, pp. 717, 718).

**To arouse the people of God**—"Satan leads many to believe that prayer to God is useless and but a form. He well knows how needful are meditation and prayer to keep Christ's followers aroused to resist his cunning and deception" (*Testimonies for the Church,* vol. 1, p. 295).

**To overcome temptation**—"All are accountable for their actions while in this world upon probation. All have power to control their actions if they will. If they are weak in virtue and purity of thoughts and acts, they can obtain help from the Friend of the helpless. Jesus is acquainted with all the weaknesses of human nature, and, if entreated, will give strength to overcome the most powerful temptations. All can obtain this strength if they seek for it in humility" (*Child Guidance*, pp. 466, 467).

**To rule the tongue**—"Sincere repentance before God will be accepted. When about to speak passionately, close your mouth. Don't utter a word. Pray before you speak, and heavenly angels will come to your assistance and drive back the evil angels, who would lead you to dishonor God, reproach His cause, and weaken your own soul" (*Testimonies for the Church*, vol. 2, p. 82).

*- Chapter Forty-four -*

# When Prayer Is Presumptuous

**Presumption defined**—"Presumption is Satan's counterfeit of faith. Faith claims God's promises, and brings forth fruit in obedience. Presumption also claims the promises, but uses them as Satan did, to excuse transgression. Faith would have led our first parents to trust the love of God, and to obey His commands. Presumption led them to transgress His law, believing that His great love would save them from the consequence of their sin" (*The Desire of Ages*, p. 126).

"That so-called faith in Christ which professes to release men from the obligation of obedience to God, is not faith, but presumption" (*Steps to Christ*, p. 61).

"It is presumption to indulge in suppositions and theories regarding matters that God has not made known to us in His Word. We need not enter into speculation regarding our future state" (*Selected Messages*, book 1, p. 173).

**A common temptation**—"Presumption is a common temptation, and as Satan assails men with this, he obtains the victory nine times out of ten. Those who profess to be followers of Christ, and claim by their faith to be enlisted in the warfare against all evil in their nature, frequently plunge without thought into temptations from which it would require a miracle to bring them forth unsullied.... The promises of God are not for us rashly to claim while we rush on recklessly into danger.... This is the most flagrant presumption" (*Testimonies for the Church*, vol. 4, pp. 44, 45).

**Satan tempted Christ on presumption**—"He then urged Christ to give him one more proof of His entire dependence upon God, one more evidence of His faith that He was the Son of God, by casting Himself from the temple....

"The Redeemer of the world would not, at Satan's suggestion, tempt God by presumptuously experimenting on His providence" (*Selected Messages,* book 1, p. 282).

"He refused to presume upon the mercy of His Father by placing Himself in peril that would make it necessary for His heavenly Father to display His power to save Him from danger" (*Selected Messages,* book 1, p. 283).

**Presumption in prayer**—"To claim that prayer will always be answered in the very way and for the particular thing that we desire, is presumption" (*Steps to Christ,* p. 96).

**Balaam's presumption**—"He did not seek to do the will of God, but chose his own course, and then endeavored to secure the sanction of the Lord.

"There are thousands at the present day who are pursuing a similar course. They would have no difficulty in understanding their duty if it were in harmony with their inclinations....But because these evidences are contrary to their desires and inclinations, they frequently set them aside and presume to go to God to learn their duty" (*Patriarchs and Prophets*, pp. 440, 441).

- *Chapter Forty-five* -

# *Prayer and Public Worship*

**Sense that God is present**—"There should be intelligent knowledge of how to come to God in reverence and godly fear with devotional love" (*Selected Messages,* book 2, p. 315).

"True reverence for God is inspired by a sense of His infinite greatness and a realization of His presence. With this sense of the Unseen, every heart should be deeply impressed. The hour and place of prayer are sacred, because God is there" (*Prophets and Kings,* pp. 48, 49).

**Kneel whenever possible**—"Both in public and in private worship it is our duty to bow down upon our knees before God when we offer our petitions to Him. This act shows our dependence upon God" (*Selected Messages,* book 2, p. 312).

***Speak God's name with reverence***—"Some think it a mark of humility to pray to God in a common manner, as if talking with a human being. They profane His name by needlessly and irreverently mingling with their prayers the words 'God Almighty,' awful, sacred words, which should never pass the lips except in subdued tones and with a feeling of awe" (*Gospel Workers,* p. 176).

***Use simple language***—"High-flown language is inappropriate in prayer, whether the petition be offered in the pulpit, in the family circle, or in secret. Especially should the one offering the public prayer use simple language, that others may understand what is said and unite with the petition.

"It is the heartfelt prayer of faith that is heard in heaven and answered on earth....

"With simplicity we should state our needs to the Lord, and claim His promise with such faith that those in the congregation will know that we have learned to prevail with God in prayer" (*Gospel Workers,* p. 177).

***Substance of our prayers***—"In our devotional meetings, our voices should express by prayer and praise our adoration of the heavenly Father, that all may know that we worship God in simplicity and truth, and in the beauty of holiness" (*Counsels to Parents, Teachers, and Students*, p. 245).

"We should not come to the house of God to pray for our families unless deep feeling shall lead us while the Spirit of God is convicting them. Generally, the proper place to pray for our families is at the family altar.... When in the house of God, we should pray for a present blessing, and should expect God to hear and answer our prayers" (*Testimonies for the Church,* vol. 1, pp. 145, 146).

***Length***—"The prayers offered in public should be short and to the point.... A few minutes is long enough for any ordinary public petition" (*Gospel Workers,* p. 175).

*- Chapter Forty-six -*

# *Family Worship*

***Heavenly presence***—"Morning and evening the heavenly universe beholds every household that prays, and the angel with the incense, representing the blood of the atonement, finds access to God" (*S.D.A. Bible Commentary*, vol. 7, p. 971; Ms. 15, 1897).

***Protection promised***—"In every Christian home God should be honored by the morning and evening sacrifices of prayer and praise....It is the duty of Christian parents, morning and evening, by earnest prayer and persevering faith, to make a hedge about their children" (*Counsels to Parents, Teachers, and Students*, p. 110).

"Will the Lord of heaven pass by such homes, and leave no blessing there? Nay, verily. Ministering angels will guard the children who are thus dedicated to God" (*Counsels to Parents, Teachers, and Students*, p. 110).

***Tragedy of a prayerless home***—"I know of nothing that causes me so great sadness as a prayerless home. I do not feel safe in such a house for a single night; and were it not for the hope of helping the parents to realize their necessity and their sad neglect, I would not remain. The children show the result of neglect, for the fear of God is not before them" (*Child Guidance*, p. 518).

***Family worship should be a daily matter***—"Family worship should not be governed by circumstances. You are not to pray occasionally, and when you have a large day's work, neglect it. In thus doing you lead your children to look upon prayer as of no special consequence....

"It should be a pleasure to worship the Lord" (*My Life Today,* p. 29).

***How to conduct family worship where there are children***—"Let the father select a portion of Scripture that is interesting and easily understood....Questions may be asked, a few earnest, interesting remarks made, or incidents, short and to the point, may be brought in by way of illustration. At least a few verses of spirited song may be sung, and the prayer offered should be short and pointed....Let all join in the Bible reading and learn and often repeat God's law. It will add to the interest of the children if they are sometimes permitted to select the reading. Question them upon it, and let them ask questions" (*Child Guidance*, pp. 521, 522).

- *Chapter Forty-seven* -

# *Morning and Evening Prayer*

***So much needed***—"Christ was the foundation of the whole Jewish economy. In the service of the Jewish priesthood we are continually reminded of the sacrifice and intercession of Christ. All who come to Christ today are to remember that His merit is the incense that mingles with the prayers of those who repent of their sins and receive pardon and mercy and grace. Our need of Christ's intercession is constant. Day by day, morning and evening, the humble heart needs to offer up prayers to which will be returned answers of grace and peace and joy. 'By him therefore let us offer the sacrifice of praise to God continually, that is, the fruit of our lips giving thanks to his name. But to do good and to communicate forget not: for with such sacrifice God is well pleased'" (*S.D.A. Bible Commentary*, vol. 6, p. 1078; Ms. 14, 1901).

*A thank offering to God*—"In every family there should be fixed times for morning and evening worship. How appropriate it is for parents to gather their children about them before the fast is broken, to thank the heavenly Father for His protection during the night, and to ask Him for His help and guidance and watch care during the day! How fitting, also, when evening comes, for parents and children to gather once more before Him and thank Him for the blessings of the day that is past!" (*Child Guidance*, p. 520).

*Faithfully done for thousands of years*—"As the priests morning and evening entered the holy place at the time of incense, the daily sacrifice was ready to be offered upon the altar in the court without. This was a time of intense interest to the worshipers who assembled at the tabernacle. Before entering into the presence of God through the ministration of the priest, they were to engage in earnest searching of heart and confession of sin. They united in silent prayer, with their faces toward the holy place. Thus their petitions ascended with the cloud of incense, while faith laid hold upon the merits of the promised Saviour prefigured by the atoning sacrifice. The hours appointed for the morning and the evening sacrifice were regarded as sacred, and they came to be observed as the set time for worship throughout the Jewish nation. And when in later times the Jews were scattered as captives in distant lands, they still at the appointed hour turned their faces toward Jerusalem and offered up their petitions to the God of Israel. In this custom Christians have an example for morning and evening prayer. While God condemns a mere round of ceremonies, without the spirit of worship, He looks with great pleasure upon those who love Him, bowing morning and evening to seek pardon for sins committed and to present their requests for needed blessings" (*Patriarchs and Prophets*, pp. 353, 354).

*Morning and evening dedication*—"Your home is a little world of itself.... You are the ones who must decide whether your children shall choose the service of God or the service of mammon, eternal life or eternal death....

"Like the patriarchs of old, those who profess to love God should erect an altar to Him wherever they pitch their tent.... Let the father, as priest of the household, lay upon the altar of God the morning and evening sacrifice, while the wife and children unite in prayer and praise. In such a household Jesus will love to abide.

"From every Christian home a holy light should shine forth. Love should be revealed in every act. It should flow out in all home intercourse, showing itself in thoughtful kindness, in gentle, unselfish courtesy. There are homes where this principle is carried out homes where God is worshiped and truest love reigns. From these homes morning and evening prayer ascends to God as sweet incense, and His mercies and blessings descend upon the suppliants like morning dew" (*My Life Today,* p. 33).

*Earnest prayer morning and evening*—"In following Christ, looking unto Him who is the Author and Finisher of your faith, you will feel that you are working under His eye, that you are influenced by His presence, and that He knows your motives. At every step you will humbly inquire: Will this please Jesus? Will it glorify God? Morning and evening your earnest prayers should ascend to God for His blessing and guidance. True prayer takes hold upon Omnipotence and gives us the victory. Upon his knees the Christian obtains strength to resist temptation" (*Testimonies for the Church,* vol. 4, pp. 615, 616).

*Keep this in mind*—"I was shown the necessity of opening the doors of our houses and hearts to the Lord. When we begin to work in earnest for ourselves and for our families, then we shall have help from God. I was shown that merely observing the Sabbath and praying morning and evening are not positive evidences that we are Christians. These outward forms may all be strictly observed, and yet true godliness be lacking. Titus 2:14. 'Who gave Himself for us, that He might redeem us from all iniquity, and purify unto Himself a peculiar people, zealous of good works.' All who profess to be Christ's followers should have command of their own spirit, not allowing themselves to speak fretfully or impatiently. The husband and father should check that inpatient word he is about to utter. He should study the effect of his words, lest they leave sadness and a blight" (*Testimonies for the Church,* vol. 1, pp. 305, 306).

- Chapter Forty-eight -

# The Mid-week Prayer Meeting

*Faithful to their duty*—"Seek every opportunity to go where prayer is wont to be made. Those who are really seeking for communion with God will be seen in the prayer meeting, faithful to do their duty and earnest and anxious to reap all the benefits they can gain. They will improve every opportunity of placing themselves where they can receive the rays of light from heaven" (*Steps to Christ,* p. 98).

***Spirit-filled Christians seen in prayer meeting***—"When the Spirit of God shall work upon the heart, cleansing the soul-temple of its defilement of worldliness and pleasure-loving, all will be seen in the prayer meeting, faithful to do their duty and earnest and anxious to reap all the benefit they can gain" (*Testimonies for the Church*, vol. 4, p. 461).

***Educate mind to love prayer meeting***—"Prepare for eternity with such zeal as you have not yet manifested. Educate your mind to love the Bible, to love the prayer meeting, to love the hour of meditation, and, above all, the hour when the soul communes with God. Become heavenly-minded if you would unite with the heavenly choir in the mansions above" (*Testimonies for the Church*, vol. 2, p. 268).

***The object of the prayer meeting***—"What is the object of assembling together? Is it to inform God, to instruct Him by telling Him all we know in prayer? We meet together to edify one another by an interchange of thoughts and feelings, to gather strength, and light, and courage by becoming acquainted with one another's hopes and aspirations; and by our earnest, heartfelt prayers, offered up in faith, we receive refreshment and vigor from the Source of our strength. These meetings should be most precious seasons and should be made interesting to all who have any relish for religious things" (*Testimonies for the Church*, vol. 2, p. 578).

***Making prayer meeting interesting***—"Our prayer and social meetings should be seasons of special help and encouragement. Each one has a work to do to make these gatherings as interesting and profitable as possible. This can best be done by having a fresh experience daily in the things of God, and by not hesitating to speak of His love in the assemblies of His people" (*Christian Service*, p. 211).

"Long, prosy talks and prayers are out of place anywhere, and especially in the social meeting.... They weary the angels and the people who listen to them. Our prayers should be short and right to the point" (*Testimonies for the Church*, vol. 4, pp. 70, 71).

***Pray short prayers***—"All should feel it a Christian duty to pray short. Tell the Lord just what you want" (*Testimonies for the Church*, vol. 2, p. 578).

"One or two minutes is long enough for any ordinary prayer" (*Testimonies for the Church*, vol. 2, p. 581).

# Chapter Forty-nine

# *Pray Wholeheartedly*

***The spirit of wrestling prayer***—"There is need of prayer, most earnest, fervent, agonizing prayer, such as David offered when he exclaimed: 'As the hart panteth after the water brooks, so panteth my soul after Thee, O God.' 'I have longed after Thy precepts.' 'I have longed for Thy salvation.' 'My soul longeth, yea, even fainteth for the courts of the Lord: my heart and my flesh crieth out for the living God.' 'My soul breaketh for the longing that it hath unto Thy judgments.' [Psalms 42:1; 119:40, 174; 84:2; 119:20.] This is the spirit of wrestling prayer, such as was possessed by the royal psalmist" (*Testimonies for the Church,* vol. 4, p. 534).

***We must learn to pray with great earnestness***—"When with earnestness and intensity we breathe a prayer in the name of Christ, there is in that very intensity a pledge from God that he is about to answer our prayer 'exceeding abundantly above all that we ask or think'" (*Christ's Object Lessons*, p. 147).

***Intense earnestness***—"God will be to us everything we will let Him be. Our languid, halfhearted prayers will not bring us returns from heaven. Oh, we need to press our petitions! Ask in faith, wait in faith, receive in faith, rejoice in hope, for everyone that seeketh findeth. Be in earnest in the matter. Seek God with all the heart.... With intense earnestness learn the trade of seeking the rich blessings that God has promised, and with persevering, determined effort you shall have His light and His truth and His rich grace" (*Our High Calling*, p. 131).

***How to face temptation and trial***—"When temptations and trials rush in upon us, let us go to God and agonize with Him in prayer. He will not turn us away empty, but will give us grace and strength to overcome, and to break the power of the enemy" (*Early Writings*, p. 46).

***Gaining the greatest victories***—"The greatest victories to the church of Christ or to the individual Christian are not those that are gained by talent or education, by wealth or the favor of men. They are those victories that are gained in the audience chamber with God, when earnest, agonizing faith lays hold upon the mighty arm of power" (*Patriarchs and Prophets*, p. 203).

***In the future crisis***—"The season of distress and anguish before us will require a faith that can endure weariness, delay, and hunger a faith that will not faint though severely tried....Those who are unwilling to deny self, to agonize before God, to pray long and earnestly for His blessing, will not obtain it" (*The Great Controversy,* p. 621).

- Chapter Fifty -

# Watch Unto Prayer

***Watch unto prayer***—"Watch unto prayer. In this way alone can you put your whole being into the Lord's work. Self must be put in the background. Those who make self prominent gain an education that soon becomes second nature to them; and they will soon fail to realize that instead of uplifting Jesus they uplift themselves" (*Counsels on Health,* p. 560).

***Watch by working***—"We cannot depend upon form or external machinery. What we need is the quickening influence of the Holy Spirit of God. 'Not by might, nor by power, but by My Spirit, saith the Lord of hosts.' Pray without ceasing, and watch by working in accordance with your prayers. As you pray, believe, trust in God. It is the time of the latter rain, when the Lord will give largely of His Spirit. Be fervent in prayer, and watch in the Spirit" (*Testimonies to Ministers and Gospel Workers,* p. 512).

***The lesson of David***—"God intended the history of David's fall to serve as a warning that even those whom He has greatly blessed and favored are not to feel secure and neglect watchfulness and prayer. And thus it has proved to those who in humility have sought to learn the lesson that God designed to teach. From generation to generation thousands have thus been led to realize their own danger from the tempter's power. The fall of David, one so greatly honored by the Lord, has awakened in them distrust of self. They have felt that God alone could keep them by His power through faith. Knowing that in Him was their strength and safety, they have feared to take the first step on Satan's ground" (*Patriarchs and Prophets,* p. 724).

***The lesson of Solomon***—"What a lesson for all who desire to save their souls to watch unto prayer continually! What a warning to keep the grace of Christ ever in their heart, to battle with inward corruptions and outward temptations!" (*S.D.A. Bible Commentary,* vol. 2, p. 1032).

***Watch lest crowded out***—"You need to watch, lest the busy activities of life lead you to neglect prayer when you most need the strength prayer would give. Godliness is in danger of being crowded out of the soul through overdevotion to business. It is a great evil to defraud the soul of the strength and heavenly wisdom which are waiting your demand. You need that illumination which God alone can give. No one is fitted to transact his business unless he has this wisdom" (*Testimonies for the Church,* vol. 5, p. 560).

*Watchful and prayerful*—"The young are ignorant of the many dangers to which they are daily exposed. They can never fully know them all; but if they are watchful and prayerful, God will keep their consciences sensitive and their perceptions clear, that they may discern the workings of the enemy and be fortified against his attacks" (*Testimonies for the Church,* vol. 3, p. 373).

*Safeguard to purity*—"Till the conflict is ended, there will be those who will depart from God, Satan will so shape circumstances that unless we are kept by divine power, they will almost imperceptibly weaken the fortifications of the soul. We need to inquire at every step, 'Is this the way of the Lord?' So long as life shall last, there will be need of guarding the affections and the passions with a firm purpose. Not one moment can we be secure except as we rely upon God, the life hidden with Christ. Watchfulness and prayer are the safeguards of purity" (*Prophets and Kings,* pp. 83, 84).

*Not watching and praying*—"They do not see the importance of self-knowledge and self-control. They do not watch and pray, lest they enter into temptation. If they would watch, they would become acquainted with their weak points, where they are most likely to be assailed by temptation. With watchfulness and prayer their weakest points can be so guarded as to become their strongest points, and they can encounter temptation without being overcome" (*Testimonies for the Church,* vol. 2, p. 511).

*Divine comfort in*—"There are many who become restless when they cannot know the definite outcome of affairs. They cannot endure uncertainty, and in their impatience they refuse to wait to see the salvation of God. Apprehended evils drive them nearly distracted. They give way to their rebellious feelings, and run hither and thither in passionate grief, seeking intelligence concerning that which has not been revealed. If they would but trust in God, and watch, they would find divine consolation. Their spirit would be calmed by communion with God. The weary and the heavy-laden would find rest unto their souls if they would only go to Jesus; but when they neglect the means that God has ordained for their comfort, and resort to other sources, hoping to learn what God has withheld, they commit the error of Saul, and thereby gain only a knowledge of evil" (*Patriarchs and Prophets*, p. 687).

# Chapter Fifty-one

# *Watch and Pray*

***Time is short***—"The great conflict that Satan created in the heavenly courts is soon, very soon, to be forever decided....Now, as never before, Satan is exercising his deceiving power to mislead and to destroy every unguarded soul" (*Testimonies for the Church,* vol. 7, p. 141).

***Satan's methods***—"When he finds himself foiled upon one point he takes new ground and fresh tactics, and tries again, working wonders in order to deceive and destroy the children of men. The youth should be carefully warned against his power....They should be led to cling to the Word of God and give attention to counsel and advice" (*Testimonies for the Church,* vol. 4, p. 212).

***Tested individually***—"Satan is to make most powerful efforts...in the last great conflict....The faith of individual members of the church will be tested as though there were not another person in the world" (*S.D.A. Bible Commentary*, vol. 7, p. 983).

***Evil angels assist***—"He [Satan] has legions of evil angels that he sends to every point where light from heaven is shining upon the people. Here he stations his pickets to seize every unguarded man, woman, or child and press them into his service" (*Testimonies for the Church,* vol. 4, p. 210).

***Constantly on guard***—"Let every soul be on the alert....Be vigilant, watching diligently lest some carefully concealed and masterly snare shall take you unawares.... Unless we are constantly on guard we shall fall an easy prey to his unnumbered deceptions" (*Testimonies for the Church*, vol. 8, pp. 99, 100).

***A comforting assurance***—"Satan leads many to believe that prayer to God is useless and but a form. He well knows how needful are meditation and prayer to keep Christ's followers aroused to resist his cunning and deception" (*Testimonies for the Church,* vol. 1, p. 295).

"The prayer of faith is the great strength of the Christian and will assuredly prevail against Satan" (*Testimonies for the Church,* vol. 1, p. 296).

***Walk prayerfully***—"The enemy cannot overcome the humble learner of Christ, the one who walks prayerfully before the Lord....

"Had Satan been suffered to have his way, there would have been no hope for Peter. He would have made complete shipwreck of faith. But the enemy dare not go one hairbreadth beyond his appointed sphere. There is no power in the whole satanic force that can disable the soul that trusts, in simple confidence, in the wisdom that comes from God" (*My Life Today,* p. 316).

- Chapter Fifty-two -

# Watch Therefore

*Keep looking up*—"A company was presented before me....They were waiting and watching. Their eyes were directed heavenward, and the words of their Master were upon their lips: 'What I say unto you, I say unto all, Watch'" (*Testimonies for the Church*, vol. 2, p. 192).

"I saw that it was impossible to have the affections and interests engrossed in worldly cares, to be increasing earthly possessions, and yet be in a waiting, watching position, as our Saviour has commanded" (*Testimonies for the Church*, vol. 2, p. 193).

*Watch the symptom*—"Watch, brethren, the first dimming of your light, the first neglect of prayer, the first symptom of spiritual slumber" (*Testimonies for the Church,* vol. 4, p. 124).

*Other things to watch*—"Watch, lest you should speak hastily, fretfully, and impatiently. Watch, lest pride should find a place in your heart. Watch, lest evil passions should overcome you, instead of you subduing them. Watch, lest...you... become light and trifling, and your influence savor of death, rather than life" (*The Faith I Live By*, p. 224).

*Watch unto prayer*—"We are to pray and watch unto prayer, that there may be no inconsistency in our lives. We must not fail to show others that we understand that watching unto prayer means living our prayers before God, that He may answer them" (*Selected Messages,* book 1, pp. 116, 117).

*Be ready for Christ's coming*—"We should watch and work and pray as though this were the last day that would be granted us. How intensely earnest, then, would be our life. How closely would we follow Jesus in all our words and deeds" (*Testimonies for the Church,* vol. 5, p. 200).

"'Pray always;' that is, be ever in the spirit of prayer, and then you will be in readiness for your Lord's coming" (*Testimonies for the Church,* vol. 5, p. 235).

**The science of your labor**—"To every worker I would say: Go forth in humble faith, and the Lord will go with you. But watch unto prayer. This is the science of your labor. The power is of God. Work in dependence upon Him, remembering that you are laborers together with Him. He is your Helper. Your strength is from Him. He will be your wisdom, your righteousness, your sanctification, your redemption. Wear the yoke of Christ, daily learning of Him, His meekness and lowliness. He will be your Comfort, your Rest" (*Testimonies for the Church,* vol. 7, p. 272).

**Watch – Watch – Watch**—"'Watch ye and pray, lest ye enter into temptation.' Mark 14:38. Watch against the stealthy approach of the enemy, watch against old habits and natural inclinations, lest they assert themselves; force them back, and watch. Watch the thoughts, watch the plans, lest they become self-centered. Watch over the souls whom Christ has purchased with His own blood. Watch for opportunities to do them good" (*Testimonies for the Church*, vol. 6, p. 410).

- Chapter Fifty-three -

# Wrestling With God

**We need to do it**—"God's faithful messengers are to seek to carry forward the Lord's work in His appointed way. They are to place themselves in close connection with the Great Teacher, that they may be daily taught of God. They are to wrestle with God in earnest prayer for a baptism of the Holy Spirit that they may meet the needs of a world perishing in sin. All power is promised those who go forth in faith to proclaim the everlasting gospel. As the servants of God bear to the world a living message fresh from the throne of glory, the light of truth will shine forth as a lamp that burneth, reaching to all parts of the world. Thus the darkness of error and unbelief will be dispelled from the minds of the honest in heart in all lands, who are now seeking after God, 'If haply they might feel after Him, and find Him'" (*Testimonies to Ministers and Gospel Workers,* pp. 459, 460).

**Will we do it?**—"Will we carry forward the work in the Lord's way? Are we willing to be taught of God? Will we wrestle with God in prayer? Will we receive the baptism of the Holy Spirit? This is what we need and may have at this time. Then we shall go forth with a message from the Lord, and the light of truth will shine forth as a lamp that burneth, reaching to all parts of the world. If we will walk humbly with God, God will walk with us. Let us humble our souls before Him, and we shall see of

His salvation" (*Fundamentals of Christian Education*, p. 532; also read *Testimonies for the Church,* vol. 8, p. 46).

***Wrestling – the great church problem solver*—**"I saw what these yearly gatherings might be, and what they should be meetings of earnest labor. Ministers should seek a heart preparation before entering upon the work of helping others, for the people are far in advance of many of the ministers. They should untiringly wrestle in prayer until the Lord blesses them. When the love of God is burning on the altar of their hearts, they will not preach to exhibit their own smartness, but to present Christ who taketh away the sins of the world.

"In the early church Christianity was taught in its purity; its precepts were given by the voice of inspiration; its ordinances were uncorrupted by the device of men. The church revealed the spirit of Christ and appeared beautiful in its simplicity. Its adorning was the holy principles and exemplary lives of its members. Multitudes were won to Christ, not by display or learning, but by the power of God which attended the plain preaching of His word. But the church has become corrupt" (*Testimonies for the Church,* vol. 5, p. 166).

*- Chapter Fifty-four -*

# Praying in Groups

***Let small companies assemble*—**"Let small companies assemble in the evening, at noon, or in the early morning to study the Bible. Let them have a season of prayer, that they may be strengthened, enlightened, and sanctified by the Holy Spirit. This work Christ wants to have done in the heart of every worker. If you yourselves will open the door to receive it, a great blessing will come to you. Angels of God will be in your assembly. You will feed upon the leaves of the tree of life. What testimonies you may bear of the loving acquaintance made with your fellow workers in these precious seasons when seeking the blessing of God. Let each tell his experience in simple words" (*Testimonies for the Church,* vol. 7, p. 195).

***Praying for the baptism of the Holy Spirit*—**"Why do we not hunger and thirst for the gift of the Spirit, since this is the means by which we are to receive power? Why do we not talk of it, pray for it, preach concerning it? The Lord is more willing to give the Holy Spirit to us than parents are to give good gifts to their children. For the baptism of the Spirit every worker should be pleading with God. Companies should be gathered together to ask for special help, for heavenly wisdom, that they may know how to plan and execute wisely" (*Testimonies for the Church*, vol. 8, p. 22).

*The praying ones in the shaking time*—"As the praying ones continued their earnest cries, at times a ray of light from Jesus came to them, to encourage their hearts and light up their countenances. Some, I saw, did not participate in this work of agonizing and pleading. They seemed indifferent and careless. They were not resisting the darkness around them, and it shut them in like a thick cloud. The angels of God left these and went to the aid of the earnest, praying ones. I saw angels of God hasten to the assistance of all who were struggling with all their power to resist the evil angels and trying to help themselves by calling upon God with perseverance. But His angels left those who made no effort to help themselves and I lost sight of them.

"I asked the meaning of the shaking I had seen and was shown that it would be caused by the straight testimony called forth by the counsel of the True Witness to the Laodiceans" (*Early Writings*, p. 270).

*Spending time together in prayer*—"We must be much in prayer if we would make progress in the divine life. When the message of truth was first proclaimed, how much we prayed....Frequently we spent hours in earnest prayer....Our perils are greater now than then" (*Testimonies for the Church,* vol. 5, pp. 161, 162).

- Chapter Fifty-five -

# Seeking God's Guidance

*Praying for guidance*—"A knowledge of truth depends not so much upon strength of intellect as upon pureness of purpose, the simplicity of an earnest, dependent faith. To those who in humility of heart seek for divine guidance, angels of God draw near. The Holy Spirit is given to open to them the rich treasures of the truth" (*Christ's Object Lessons*, p. 59).

*Helpful guidelines*—"You are fighting for the crown of life....Live to please Him who thought you of such value that He gave Jesus, His only begotten Son, to save you from your sins....Ever keep before you the thought that what is worth doing at all, is worth doing well. Depend upon God for wisdom, that you may not discourage one soul in right doing. Work with Christ in drawing souls to Him....Do your very best in everything you undertake. Jesus is your Saviour, and rely upon Him to help you day by day, that you may not sow tares, but the good seed of the kingdom....

"You must learn to see with your brain as well as your eyes. You must educate your judgment so that it shall not be feeble and inefficient. You must pray for guidance, and commit your way unto the Lord. You must close your heart against all foolishness and sin, and open it to every heavenly influence. You must make the most of your time and opportunities, in order to develop a symmetrical character" (*Sons and Daughters of God,* p. 283).

*Guidance by chance methods*—(Carefully read *Selected Messages,* book 2, pp. 28, 325-328.)

*Avoid uncertain tests*—"The Lord works in no haphazard way. Seek Him most earnestly in prayer. He will impress the mind, and will give tongue and utterance. The people of God are to be educated not to trust in human inventions and uncertain tests as a means of learning God's will concerning them" (*S.D.A. Bible Commentary*, vol. 6, p. 1054).

*"It is written"*—"Jesus met Satan with the words of Scripture. 'It is written,' He said....Satan demanded of Christ a miracle as a sign of His divinity. But that which is greater than all miracles, a firm reliance upon a 'Thus saith the Lord,' was a sign that could not be controverted" (*The Desire of Ages,* p. 120).

*The Word of God our guide*—"The Word of the eternal God is our guide. Through this Word we have been made wise unto salvation. This Word is ever to be in our hearts and on our lips. 'It is written' is to be our anchor. Those who make God's Word their counselor realize the weakness of the human heart....Their hearts are ever prayerful, and they have the guardianship of holy angels" (*Testimonies for the Church*, vol. 6, pp. 160, 161).

*Unsafe guides*—"Impressions and feelings are no sure evidence that a person is led by the Lord. Satan will, if he is unsuspected, give feelings and impressions. These are not safe guides. All should thoroughly acquaint themselves with the evidences of our faith, and the great study should be how they can adorn their profession and bear fruit to the glory of God" (*Testimonies for the Church,* vol. 1, p. 413).

*No human device or plan*—"There is no chance work with God in the directing of His people. Let us never forget that His providences guide in every circumstance of life, and that in the determination of important questions regarding His work and people there is no uncertainty....

"Our faith in Christ is not to be exchanged for any human device or plan. Those who have faith in Him…will never resort to the game of chance for an understanding of their duty. God is not glorified by such experiments" (*The Unwise Use of Money and the Spirit of Speculation*, pp. 38, 39).

**Christ was guided by God's will**—"Before He came to earth, the plan lay out before Him, perfect in all its details. But as He walked among men, He was guided, step by step, by the Father's will. He did not hesitate to act at the appointed time. With the same submission He waited until the time had come" (*The Desire of Ages,* p. 147).

**Warnings**—"With some the evil has revealed itself in the form of man-made tests for ascertaining a knowledge of the will of God; and I was shown that this was a delusion which became infatuation, and that it is contrary to the will of the Lord" (*Selected Messages,* book 2, p. 28).

**Pray for divine guidance**—"In the crowds of the street, in the midst of a business engagement, we may send up a petition to God and plead for divine guidance" (*Steps to Christ,* p. 99).

**The will of God is expressed in His law**—"God will draw near to every seeking soul" (*Selected Messages,* book 1, p. 116).

"The will of God is expressed in the precepts of His holy law, and the principles of this law are the principles of heaven. The angels of heaven attain unto no higher knowledge than to know the will of God, and to do His will is the highest service that can engage their powers" (*Thoughts from the Mount of Blessing,* p. 109).

**Three ways in which God's will is revealed**—"There are three ways in which the Lord reveals His will to us, to guide us, and to fit us to guide others. How may we know His voice from that of a stranger? How shall we distinguish it from the voice of a false shepherd? God reveals His will to us in His Word, the Holy Scriptures. His voice is also revealed in His providential workings; and it will be recognized if we do not separate our souls from Him by walking in our own ways, doing according to our own wills, and following the promptings of an unsanctified heart, until the senses have become so confused that eternal things are not discerned, and the voice of Satan is so disguised that it is accepted as the voice of God.

"Another way in which God's voice is heard is through the appeals of His Holy Spirit, making impressions upon the heart, which will be brought out in the character. If you are in doubt upon any subject you must first consult the Scriptures. If you have truly begun the life of faith you have given yourself to the Lord to be wholly His, and He has taken you to mold and fashion according to His purpose, that you may be a vessel unto honor" (*Testimonies for the Church,* vol. 5, p. 512).

**Dedication and obedience required**—"But many are attracted by the beauty of Christ and the glory of heaven, who yet shrink from the conditions by which alone these can become their own....They look toward the narrow way and the strait gate; but selfish pleasure, love of the world, pride, unsanctified ambition, place a barrier between them and the Saviour....They desire the good, they make some effort to obtain it; but they do not choose it; they have not a settled purpose to secure it at the cost of all things" (*Thoughts from the Mount of Blessing,* p. 143).

**Faith united with prayer**—"True faith and true prayer...are as two arms by which the human suppliant lays hold upon the power of Infinite Love. Faith is trusting in God, believing that He loves us, and knows what is for our best good. Thus, instead of our own way, it leads us to choose His way" (*Gospel Workers,* p. 259).

- *Chapter Fifty-six* -

# What to Pray For

**Ask for anything He has promised**—"Every promise in the word of God furnishes us with subject matter for prayer, presenting the pledged word of Jehovah as our assurance. Whatever spiritual blessing we need, it is our privilege to claim through Jesus. We may tell the Lord, with the simplicity of a child, exactly what we need. We may state to Him our temporal matters, asking Him for bread and raiment as well as for the bread of life and the robe of Christ's righteousness. Your heavenly Father knows that you have need of all these things, and you are invited to ask Him concerning them. It is through the name of Jesus that every favor is received. God will honor that name, and will supply your necessities from the riches of His liberality" (*Thoughts from the Mount of Blessing,* p. 133).

**Ask for nourishment**—"When we pray, 'Give us this day our daily bread,' we ask for others as well as ourselves. And we acknowledge that what God gives us is not for ourselves alone. God gives to us in trust, that we may feed the hungry....

"The prayer for daily bread includes not only food to sustain the body, but that spiritual bread which will nourish the soul unto life everlasting" (*Thoughts from the Mount of Blessing,* pp. 111, 112).

*For your own necessities*—"Every soul has the privilege of stating to the Lord his own special necessities and to offer his individual thanksgiving for the blessings that he daily receives" (*Testimonies for the Church*, vol. 9, pp. 278, 279).

*For the cause of God*—"The varied interests of the cause furnish us with food for reflection and inspiration for our prayers" (*Testimonies for the Church*, vol. 4, p. 459).

*For the Holy Spirit*—"There is now need of much prayer....The dispensation in which we are now living is to be, to those who ask, the dispensation of the Holy Spirit. Ask for His blessing. It is time we were more intense in our devotion....The Lord expects us to ask Him" (*Testimonies to Ministers and Gospel Workers*, pp. 511, 512).

*For power and wisdom*—"As you ask the Lord to help you, honor your Saviour by believing that you do receive His blessing. All power, all wisdom, are at our command. We have only to ask" (*The Ministry of Healing*, p. 514).

"We must seek wisdom from on high that we may stand in this day of error and delusion" (*Early Writings*, pp. 87, 88).

*For an understanding of God's Word*—"No man is safe for a day or an hour without prayer. Especially should we entreat the Lord for wisdom to understand His Word. Here are revealed the wiles of the tempter and the means by which he may be successfully resisted. Satan is an expert in quoting Scripture, placing his own interpretation upon passages, by which he hopes to cause us to stumble" (*The Great Controversy*, p. 530).

*For an understanding of these times*—"Pray most earnestly for an understanding of the times in which we live, for a fuller conception of His purpose, and for increased efficiency in soul-saving" (*Selected Messages*, book 2, p. 400).

*Ask for fresh supplies of grace*—"Those who at Pentecost were endued with power from on high, were not thereby freed from further temptation and trial. As they witnessed for truth and righteousness they were repeatedly assailed by the enemy of all truth, who sought to rob them of their Christian experience. They were compelled to strive with all their God-given powers to reach the measure of the stature of men and women in Christ Jesus. Daily they prayed for fresh supplies of grace, that they might reach higher and still higher toward perfection. Under the Holy Spirit's working even the weakest, by exercising faith in God, learned to improve their entrusted powers and to become sanctified, refined, and ennobled. As in humility they submitted to the molding influence of the Holy Spirit, they received of the fullness of the Godhead and were fashioned in the likeness of the divine" (*The Acts of the Apostles*, pp. 49, 50).

***Ask for today's needs***—"The truth if received into the heart is able to make you wise unto salvation. In believing and obeying it you will receive grace sufficient for the duties and trials of today. Grace for tomorrow you do not need. You should feel that you have only to do with today. Overcome for today; deny self for today; watch and pray for today; obtain victories in God for today. Our circumstances and surroundings, the changes daily transpiring around us, and the written word of God which discerns and proves all things these are sufficient to teach us our duty and just what we ought to do, day by day" (*Testimonies for the Church,* vol. 3, p. 333).

*- Chapter Fifty-seven -*

# Entering the Attitude of Prayer

*(Note: You may not feel like praying, even though you know you need to do so. This will help you: Pray for repentance. Scripture reveals that a spirit of heartbroken repentance comes from God just as surely as does forgiveness. "The God of our fathers raised up Jesus, whom ye slew and hanged on a tree. Him hath God exalted with his right hand to be a Prince and a Saviour, for to give repentance to Israel, and forgiveness of sins. Acts 5:30, 31).*

***Placed in the presence of God***—"Prayer, whether offered in the public assembly, at the family altar, or in secret, places man directly in the presence of God" (*My Life Today,* p. 18).

***Have special appointed times for prayer***—"We, too, must have times set apart for meditation and prayer and for receiving spiritual refreshing. We do not value the power and efficacy of prayer as we should. Prayer and faith will do what no power on earth can accomplish" (*The Ministry of Healing,* p. 509).

***Try to be alone with Him***—"Have a place for secret prayer. Jesus had select places for communion with God, and so should we. We need often to retire to some spot, however humble, where we can be alone with God.

"In the secret place of prayer, where no eye but God's can see, no ear but His can hear, we may pour out our most hidden desires and longings" (*Thoughts from the Mount of Blessing,* p. 84).

***Read the Bible and pray over what you read***—"Prayer, oh, how is this precious privilege neglected! The reading of the Word of God prepares the mind for prayer.... Prayer is the strength of the Christian. When alone he is not alone; he feels the presence of One who has said: 'Lo, I am with you alway'" (*Testimonies for the Church,* vol. 1, p. 504).

"We should come with reverence to the study of the Bible, feeling that we are in the presence of God....Every student, as he opens the Scriptures, should ask for the enlightenment of the Holy Spirit; and the promise is sure, that it will be given" (*Testimonies to Ministers and Gospel Workers,* pp. 107, 108).

***The power of song***—"Let praise and thanksgiving be expressed in song. When tempted, instead of giving utterance to our feelings, let us by faith lift up a song of thanksgiving to God.

"Song is a weapon that we can always use against discouragement" (*The Ministry of Healing,* p. 254).

***Thinking of and praising God***—"If we would but think of God as often as we have evidence of His care for us we should keep Him ever in our thoughts and should delight to talk of Him and to praise Him" (*Steps to Christ,* p. 102).

***What to do when you don't want to pray***—"When we feel the least inclined to commune with Jesus, let us pray the most. By so doing we shall break Satan's snare, the clouds of darkness will disappear, and we shall realize the sweet presence of Jesus" (*Historical Sketches of the Foreign Missions of the Seventh-day Adventists,* p. 146).

- Chapter Fifty-eight -

# Pray for Others

***Begin at home***—"Let those who desire to work for God begin at home, in their own household, in their own neighborhood, among their own friends. Here they will find a favorable missionary field" (*Testimonies for the Church,* vol. 6, p. 428).

"In private prayer all have the privilege of praying as long as they desire and of being as explicit as they please. They can pray for all their relatives and friends" (*Testimonies for the Church,* vol. 2, p. 578).

"God has promised to give wisdom to those that ask in faith, and He will do just as He said He would. He is pleased with the faith that takes Him at His word. The mother of Augustine prayed for her son's conversion. She saw no evidence that the Spirit of God was impressing his heart, but she was not discouraged. She laid her finger upon the texts, presenting before God His own words, and pleaded as only a mother can. Her deep humiliation, her earnest importunities, her unwavering faith, prevailed, and the Lord gave her the desire of her heart. Today He is just as ready to listen to the petitions of His people" (*Testimonies for the Church,* vol. 5, pp. 322, 323).

*Praying for imperiled youth*—"When they [your children] went into the Army, your prayers followed them. They were wonderfully preserved from harm....How many prayers were lodged in heaven that these sons might be preserved to obey God, to devote their lives to His glory!" (*Testimonies for the Church*, vol. 2, p. 275; from a personal testimony to a mother after the Civil War).

*Pray and speak*—"There are many from whom hope has departed. Bring back the sunshine to them. Many have lost their courage. Speak to them words of cheer. Pray for them" (*Christ's Object Lessons*, p. 418).

*Pray, pray*—"The Lord turned the captivity of Job when he prayed, not only for himself, but for those who were opposing him. When he felt earnestly desirous that the souls that had trespassed against him might be helped, he himself received help. Let us pray, not only for ourselves, but for those who have hurt us, and are continuing to hurt us. Pray, pray, especially in your mind. Give not the Lord rest; for His ears are open to hear sincere, importunate prayers, when the soul is humbled before Him" (*S.D.A. Bible Commentary*, vol. 3, p. 1141).

*Pray for persons you visit*—"This work requires you to watch for souls as they that must give an account. The tenderness of Christ must pervade the heart of the worker. If you have a love for souls you will reveal a tender solicitude for them. You will offer humble, earnest, heartfelt prayers for those whom you visit. The fragrance of Christ's love will be revealed in your work. He who gave His own life for the life of the world will co-operate with the unselfish worker to make an impression upon human hearts" (*Testimonies for the Church*, vol. 6, pp. 75, 76).

*Pray for people who are suffering*—"The divine Healer is present in the sick-room; He hears every word of the prayers offered to Him in the simplicity of true faith. His disciples to-day are to pray for the sick, as verily as did the disciples of old. And there will be recoveries; for 'the prayer of faith shall save the sick'" (*Gospel Workers,* p. 215).

**Wonderful results seen later**—"With unutterable love, Jesus welcomes His faithful ones to the joy of their Lord. The Saviour's joy is in seeing, in the kingdom of glory, the souls that have been saved by His agony and humiliation. And the redeemed will be sharers in His joy, as they behold, among the blessed, those who have been won to Christ through their prayers, their labors, and their loving sacrifice. As they gather about the great white throne, gladness unspeakable will fill their hearts, when they behold those whom they have won for Christ, and see that one has gained others, and these still others, all brought into the haven of rest, there to lay their crowns at Jesus' feet and praise Him through the endless cycles of eternity" (*The Great Controversy,* p. 647).

- Chapter Fifty-nine -

# God's Voice to Man

**Time to listen**—"Christ is ever sending messages to those who listen for His voice" (*The Ministry of Healing,* p. 509).

**When other voices hushed**—"When every other voice is hushed, and in quietness we wait before Him, the silence of the soul makes more distinct the voice of God" (*The Desire of Ages,* p. 363).

**God's voices in Scripture**— "The Bible is God's voice speaking to us, just as surely as though we could hear it with our ears" (*Testimonies for the Church*, vol. 6, p. 393).

"The Scriptures are to be received as God's word to us, not written merely, but spoken....

"So with all the promises of God's Word. In them He is speaking to us individually, speaking as directly as if we could listen to His voice" (*The Ministry of Healing,* p. 122).

"Never attempt to search the Scriptures unless you are ready to listen…to the Word of God as though His voice were speaking directly to you from the living Oracles" (*S.D.A. Bible Commentary*, vol. 7, p. 919).

**God's voice in duty**—"Nothing will give such clear views of self as secret prayer.... Plain, simple duties that must not be neglected will open before you" (*Testimonies for the Church,* vol. 5, p. 163).

"There is no help for man, woman, or child who will not hear and obey the voice of duty, for the voice of duty is the voice of God" (*Testimonies to Ministers and Gospel Workers,* p. 402).

**God's voice in conscience**—"Conscience is the voice of God" (*Testimonies for the Church,* vol. 5, p. 120).

"We must resist and conquer inclination, and obey the voice of conscience without parleying or compromise, lest its promptings cease, and will and impulse control" (*Selected Messages,* book 1, p. 28).

**God's voice in His Spirit**—"Another Way in which God's voice is heard is through the appeals of His Holy Spirit, making impressions upon the heart" (*Testimonies for the Church,* vol. 5, p. 512).

- *Chapter Sixty* -

# Praying in Christ's Name

**More than a mention**—"To pray in the name of Jesus is something more than a mere mention of that name at the beginning and the ending of the prayer. It is to pray in the mind and spirit of Jesus, while we believe His promises, rely upon His grace, and work His works" (*Steps to Christ,* pp. 100, 101).

**All in His name**—"The disciples were to carry their work forward in Christ's name. Their every word and act was to fasten attention on His name, as possessing that vital power by which sinners may be saved....In His name they were to present their petitions to the Father, and they would receive answer....Nothing was to be recognized in His kingdom that did not bear His name and superscription" (*The Acts of the Apostles,* p. 28).

**Ask in His name**—" 'Ask in My name,' Christ says....'This will give your prayers efficiency, and the Father will give you the riches of His grace. Wherefore ask, and ye shall receive, that your joy may be full'" (*Testimonies for the Church,* vol. 8, p. 178).

**God honors that name**—" 'If we ask anything according to His will, He heareth us: and if we know that He hear us, whatsoever we ask, we know that we have the petitions that we desired of Him.' John 5: 14, 15. Then press your petition to the Father in the name of Jesus. God will honor that name" (*Christ's Object Lessons*, p. 148).

***The secret of success***—"As yet the disciples were unacquainted with the Saviour's unlimited resources and power. He said to them, 'Hitherto have ye asked nothing in My name.' John 16:24. He explained that the secret of their success would be in asking for strength and grace in His name. He would be present before the Father to make request for them....

"There is no one living who has any power that he has not received from God, and the source whence it comes is open to the weakest human being. 'Whatsoever ye shall ask in My name,' said Jesus, 'that will I do, that the Father may be glorified in the Son.' 'If ye shall ask anything in My name, I will do it'" (*The Desire of Ages,* p. 667).

***God delights to answer***—"We must not only pray in Christ's name, but by the inspiration of the Holy Spirit. This explains what is meant when it is said that the Spirit 'maketh intercession for us, with groanings which cannot be uttered.' Romans 8:26. Such a prayer God delights to answer. When with earnestness and intensity we breathe a prayer in the name of Christ, there is in that very intensity a pledge from God that He is about to answer our prayer 'exceeding abundantly above all that we ask or think.' Ephesians 3:20" (*Christ's Object Lessons*, p. 147).

***Significance of praying in His name***—"To pray in Christ's name means much. It means that we are to accept His character, manifest His spirit, and work His works. The Saviour's promise is given on condition. 'If ye love Me,' He says, 'keep My commandments.' He saves men, not in sin, but from sin; and those who love Him will show their love by obedience" (*The Desire of Ages,* p. 668).

*- Chapter Sixty-one -*

# Our Prayers Go to Our High Priest in the Sanctuary - 1

***The third angel points to the work of Christ as our Mediator***—"I saw the incense in the censer smoke as Jesus offered their confessions and prayers to His Father. And as it ascended, a bright light rested upon Jesus and upon the mercy seat; and the earnest, praying ones, who were troubled because they had discovered themselves to be transgressors of God's law, were blessed, and their countenances lighted up with hope and joy. They joined in the work of the third angel and raised their voices to proclaim the solemn warning. But few at first received it; yet the faithful continued with energy to proclaim the message. Then I saw many embrace the message of the third angel and unite their voices with those who had first given the warning, and they honored God by observing His sanctified rest day.

"Many who embraced the third message had not had an experience in the two former messages. Satan understood this, and his evil eye was upon them to overthrow them; but the third angel was pointing them to the most holy place, and those who had had an experience in the past messages were pointing them the way to the heavenly sanctuary. Many saw the perfect chain of truth in the angels' messages, and gladly received them in their order, and followed Jesus by faith into the heavenly sanctuary. These messages were represented to me as an anchor to the people of God. Those who understand and receive them will be kept from being swept away by the many delusions of Satan" (*Early Writings*, p. 256).

***Pray to the Sanctuary***—"Do not bow down and cover up your faces as if there were something that you desired to conceal; but lift up your eyes toward the heavenly sanctuary, where Christ your Mediator stands before the Father to present your prayers, mingled with His own merit and spotless righteousness, as fragrant incense" (*Counsels to Parents, Teachers, and Students*, p. 241).

***Watched, strengthened and cared-for***—"As yet the disciples were unacquainted with the Saviour's unlimited resources and power. He said to them, 'Hitherto have ye asked nothing in My name.' John 16:24. He explained that the secret of their success would be in asking for strength and grace in His name. He would be present before the Father to make request for them. The prayer of the humble suppliant He presents as His own desire in that soul's behalf. Every sincere prayer is heard in heaven. It may not be fluently expressed; but if the heart is in it, it will ascend to the sanctuary where Jesus ministers, and He will present it to the Father without one awkward, stammering word, beautiful and fragrant with the incense of His own perfection" (*The Desire of Ages,* p. 667).

***To the Angel of the Covenant***—"God does not leave them to fight unaided against the tempter. They have an all-powerful Helper.

"Stronger far than their foe is He who in this world and in human nature met and conquered Satan, resisting every temptation that comes to the youth today. He is their Elder Brother. He feels for them a deep and tender interest. He keeps over them a constant watch-care, and He rejoices when they try to please Him. As they pray, He mingles with their prayers the incense of His righteousness, and offers them to God as a fragrant sacrifice. In His strength the youth can endure hardness as good soldiers of the cross. Strengthened with His might, they are enabled to reach the high ideals before them. The sacrifice made on Calvary is the pledge of their victory" (*Messages to Young People*, pp. 95, 96).

*To our Advocate*—"Pray, yes, pray with unshaken faith and trust. The Angel of the covenant, even our Lord Jesus Christ, is the Mediator who secures the acceptance of the prayers of His believing ones" (*Testimonies for the Church*, vol. 8, p. 179).

*The connecting link*—"The Lord did not deem the plan of salvation complete while invested only with His own love. By His appointment He has placed at His altar an Advocate clothed with our nature. As our Intercessor, Christ's office work is to introduce us to God as His sons and daughters.

"Christ has pledged Himself to be our substitute and surety, and He neglects no one. There is an inexhaustible fund of perfect obedience accruing from His obedience. In heaven His merits, His self-denial and self-sacrifice, are treasured as incense to be offered up with the prayers of His people. As the sinner's sincere, humble prayers ascend to the throne of God, Christ mingles with them the merits of His own life of perfect obedience. Our prayers are made fragrant by this incense. Christ has pledged Himself to intercede in our behalf, and the Father always hears the Son" (*Sons and Daughters of God,* p. 22).

*Through the gates*—"In Christ's name our petitions ascend to the Father. He intercedes in our behalf, and the Father lays open all the treasures of His grace for our appropriation, for us to enjoy and impart to others. 'Ask in My name,' Christ says. 'I do not say that I will pray the Father for you; for the Father Himself loveth you. Make use of My name. This will give your prayers efficiency, and the Father will give you the riches of His grace. Wherefore ask, and ye shall receive, that your joy may be full.'

"Christ is the connecting link between God and man. He has promised His personal intercession. He places the whole virtue of His righteousness on the side of the suppliant. He pleads for man, and man, in need of divine help, pleads for himself in the presence of God, using the influence of the One who gave His life for the life of the world. As we acknowledge before God our appreciation of Christ's merits, Christ places us close by His side, encircling us with His human arm, while with His divine arm He grasps the throne of the Infinite. He puts His merits, as sweet incense, in the censer in our hands, in order to encourage our petitions. He promises to hear and answer our supplications.

"Yes, Christ has become the medium of prayer between man and God. He has also become the medium of blessing between God and man. He has united divinity with humanity. Men are to co-operate with Him for the salvation of their own souls, and then make earnest, persevering efforts to save those who are ready to die" (*Testimonies for the Church*, vol. 8, p. 178).

***Through the gates***—"The simple prayers indited by the Holy Spirit will ascend through the gates ajar, the open door which Christ has declared: I have opened, and no man can shut. These prayers mingled with the incense of the perfection of Christ, will ascend as fragrance to the Father, and answers will come" (*Testimonies for the Church*, vol. 6, p. 467).

***Into the holiest***—"In the holiest I saw an ark; on the top and sides of it was purest gold. On each end of the ark was a lovely cherub, with its wings spread out over it. Their faces were turned toward each other, and they looked downward. Between the angels was a golden censer. Above the ark, where the angels stood, was an exceeding bright glory, that appeared like a throne where God dwelt. Jesus stood by the ark, and as the saints' prayers came up to Him, the incense in the censer would smoke, and He would offer up their prayers with the smoke of the incense to His Father" (*Early Writings*, p. 32).

***Fragrant incense***—"They have willingly endured hardship and privation, and have watched and prayed for the success of the work. Their gifts and sacrifices express the fervent gratitude of their hearts to Him who has called them out of darkness into His marvelous light. Their prayers and their alms come up as a memorial before God. No incense more fragrant can ascend to heaven" (*Testimonies for the Church,* vol. 7, p. 216).

***Purified incense***—"The religious services, the prayers, the praise, the penitent confession of sin ascend from true believers as incense to the heavenly sanctuary; but passing through the corrupt channels of humanity, they are so defiled that unless purified by blood, they can never be of value with God. They ascend not in spotless purity, and unless the Intercessor who is at God's right hand presents and purifies all by His righteousness, it is not acceptable to God. All incense from earthly tabernacles must be moist with the cleansing drops of the blood of Christ. He holds before the Father the censer of His own merits, in which there is no taint of earthly corruption. He gathers into this censer the prayers, the praise, and the confessions of His people, and with these He puts His own spotless righteousness. Then, perfumed with the merits of Christ's propitiation, the incense comes up before God wholly and entirely acceptable. Then gracious answers are returned" (*S.D.A. Bible Commentary*, vol. 6, p. 1078; Ms. 50, 1900).

***The intercession of Christ and the Holy Spirit***—"Christ, our Mediator, and the Holy Spirit are constantly interceding in man's behalf, but the Spirit pleads not for us as does Christ, who presents His blood, shed from the foundation of the world; the Spirit works upon our hearts, drawing out prayers and penitence, praise and thanksgiving. The gratitude which flows from our lips is the result of the Spirit's striking the cords of the soul in holy memories, awakening the music of the heart.

"Oh, that all may see that everything in obedience, in penitence, in praise and thanksgiving, must be placed upon the glowing fire of the righteousness of Christ. The fragrance of this righteousness ascends like a cloud around the mercy seat" (*Selected Messages,* book 1, p. 344).

**Incense from Christian homes**—"Like the patriarchs of old, those who profess to love God should erect an altar to the Lord wherever they pitch their tent. If ever there was a time when every house should be a house of prayer, it is now. Fathers and mothers should often lift up their hearts to God in humble supplication for themselves and their children. Let the father, as priest of the household, lay upon the altar of God the morning and evening sacrifice, while the wife and children unite in prayer and praise. In such a household Jesus will love to tarry.

"From every Christian home a holy light should shine forth. Love should be revealed in action. It should flow out in all home intercourse, showing itself in thoughtful kindness, in gentle, unselfish courtesy. There are homes where this principle is carried out homes where God is worshiped and truest love reigns. From these homes morning and evening prayer ascends to God as sweet incense, and His mercies and blessings descend upon the suppliants like the morning dew" (*Patriarchs and Prophets*, p. 144).

- Chapter Sixty-two -

# Our Prayers Go to Our High Priest in the Sanctuary - 2

**The altar of prayer**—"A well-disciplined family, who love and obey God, will be cheerful and happy. The father, when he returns from his daily labor, will not bring his perplexities to his home. He will feel that home, and the family circle, are too sacred to be marred with unhappy perplexities. When he left his home, he did not leave his Saviour and his religion behind. Both were his companions. The sweet influence of his home, the blessing of his wife, and love of his children, make his burdens light, and he returns with peace in his heart, and cheerful encouraging words for his wife and children, who are waiting to joyfully welcome his coming. As he bows with his family, at the altar of prayer, to offer up his grateful thanks to God, for His preserving care of himself and loved ones through the day, angels of God hover in the room, and bear the fervent prayers of God-fearing parents to Heaven, as sweet incense, which are answered by returning blessings" (*Selected Messages,* book 2, pp. 439, 440).

*Mingled with His merits*—"As the high priest sprinkled the warm blood upon the mercy seat while the fragrant cloud of incense ascended before God, so, while we confess our sins and plead the efficacy of Christ's atoning blood, our prayers are to ascend to heaven, fragrant with the merits of our Saviour's character. Notwithstanding our unworthiness, we are to remember that there is One who can take away sin, and who is willing and anxious to save the sinner. With His own blood He paid the penalty for all wrongdoers. Every sin acknowledged before God with a contrite heart, He will remove" (*S.D.A. Bible Commentary*, vol. 7, p. 970).

*Part of the 1888 Message*—"The efficacy of the blood of Christ was to be presented to the people with freshness and power, that their faith might lay hold upon its merits. As the high priest sprinkled the warm blood upon the mercy seat, while the fragrant cloud of incense ascended before God, so while we confess our sins and plead the efficacy of Christ's atoning blood, our prayers are to ascend to heaven, fragrant with the merits of our Saviour's character. Notwithstanding our unworthiness, we are ever to bear in mind that there is One that can take away sin and save the sinner" (*Testimonies to Ministers and Gospel Workers,* pp. 92, 93; read the entire chapter in *Testimonies to Ministers and Gospel Workers*, pp. 89-98).

*In prayer, bringing them to the Sanctuary*—"You are the agent through whom God will speak to the soul. Precious things will be brought to your remembrance, and with a heart overflowing with the love of Jesus, you will speak words of vital interest and import. Your simplicity and sincerity will be the highest eloquence, and your words will be registered in the books of heaven as fit words, which are like apples of gold in pictures of silver. God will make them a healing flood of heavenly influence, awakening conviction and desire, and Jesus will add His intercession to your prayers, and claim for the sinner the gift of the Holy Spirit, and pour it upon his soul. And there will be joy in the presence of the angels of God over one sinner that repenteth" (*Sons and Daughters of God,* p. 274).

*Beautiful colored incense*—"Two lovely cherubs, one on each end of the ark, stood with their wings outstretched above it, and touching each other above the head of Jesus as He stood before the mercy seat. Their faces were turned toward each other, and they looked downward to the ark, representing all the angelic host looking with interest at the law of God. Between the cherubim was a golden censer, and as the the prayers of the saints, offered in faith, came up to Jesus, and He presented them to His father, a cloud of fragrance arose from the incense, looking like smoke of most beautiful colors. Above the place where Jesus stood, before the ark, was exceeding bright glory that I could not look upon; it appeared like the throne of God. As the incense ascended to the Father, the excellent glory came from the throne to Jesus, and from Him it was shed upon those whose prayers had come up like sweet incense. Light poured upon Jesus in rich abundance and overshadowed the mercy seat, and the train of glory filled the temple. I could not long look upon the surpassing brightness. No language can describe it. I was overwhelmed and turned from the majesty and glory of the scene" (*Early Writings*, p. 252).

*The cloud of incense in the earthly sanctuary as they prayed*—Read *Patriarchs and Prophets,* pp. 353, 354; *The Desire of Ages*, pp. 78, 576; and *The Great Controversy*, p. 19.

*"Study His mediatorial work"*—"To the apostle John on the Isle of Patmos were revealed the things which God desired him to give to the people. Study these revelations.... Behold the life and character of Christ, and study His mediatorial work. Here is infinite wisdom, infinite love, infinite justice, infinite mercy" (*Testimonies for the Church*, vol. 6, p. 59).

*Christ is the connecting link*—"Christ is the connecting link between God and man. He has promised His personal intercession. He places the whole virtue of His righteousness on the side of the suppliant....As we approach God through the virtue of the Redeemer's merits, Christ places us close by His side, encircling us with His human arm, while with His divine arm He grasps the throne of the Infinite....He promises to hear and answer our supplications.

"Yes, Christ has become the medium of prayer between man and God. He has also become the medium of blessing between God and man" (*Testimonies for the Church*, vol. 8, p. 178).

*Jesus our representative*—" 'This is My beloved Son, in whom I am well pleased,' embraces humanity. God spoke to Jesus as our representative....The glory that rested upon Christ is a pledge of the love of God for us. It tells of the power of prayer, how the human voice may reach the ear of God, and our petitions find acceptance in the courts of heaven....The voice which spoke to Jesus says to every believing soul, 'This is My beloved child, in whom I on well pleased'" (*The Desire of Ages,* p. 113).

*Divinity united with humanity*—"The Saviour was deeply anxious for His disciples to understand for what purpose His divinity was united to humanity....

God was manifested in Him that He might be manifested in them. Jesus revealed no qualities, and exercised no powers, that men may not have through faith in Him. His perfect humanity is that which all His followers may possess, if they will be in subjection to God as He was" (*The Desire of Ages,* p. 664).

***Essential to the plan of salvation***—"The intercession of Christ in man's behalf in the sanctuary above is as essential to the plan of salvation as was His death upon the cross. By His death He began that work which after His resurrection He ascended to complete in heaven....Jesus has opened the way to the Father's throne, and through His mediation the sincere desire of all who come to Him in faith may be presented before God" (*The Great Controversy,* p. 489).

- *Chapter Sixty-three* -

# *Prayer Defeats Satan*

***The price of safety***—"In the conflict with satanic agencies there are decisive moments that determine the victory either on the side of God or on the side of the prince of this world. If those engaged in the warfare are not wide awake, earnest, vigilant, praying for wisdom, watching unto prayer,...Satan comes off victor, when he might have been vanquished by the armies of the Lord....

"Spiritual vigilance on our part individually is the price of safety. Swerve not to Satan's side a single inch, lest he gain advantage over you" (*S.D.A. Bible Commentary,* vol. 6, p. 1094; Letter 47, 1893).

"Prayer brings Jesus to our side, and gives to the fainting, perplexed soul new strength to overcome the world, the flesh, and the devil. Prayer turns aside the attacks of Satan" (*Christ's Object Lessons,* p. 250).

***Warfare against Satan lifelong***—"We have before us a warfare, a lifelong conflict with Satan and his seductive temptations. The enemy will use every argument, every deception, to entangle the soul; and in order to win the crown of life, we must put forth earnest, persevering effort" (*Messages to Young People,* p. 104).

"We must have on the whole armor of God and be ready at any moment for a conflict with the powers of darkness. When temptations and trials rush in upon us, let us go to God and agonize with Him in prayer. He will not turn us away empty, but will give us grace and strength to overcome, and to break the power of the enemy" (*Early Writings,* p. 46).

***Suppose we neglect to pray, or pray only occasionally***—"Neglect the exercise of prayer, or engage in prayer spasmodically, now and then, as seems convenient, and you lose your hold on God. The spiritual faculties lose their vitality, the religious experience lacks health and vigor" (*Gospel Workers,* p. 255).

***Beware!***—"Beware how you neglect secret prayer and a study of God's Word. These are your weapons against him who is striving to hinder your progress heavenward. The first neglect of prayer and Bible study makes easier the second neglect" (*Messages to Young People*, p. 96).

***Satan's insinuation***—"The prayer of faith is the great strength of the Christian and will assuredly prevail against Satan. This is why he insinuates that we have no need of prayer. The name of Jesus, our Advocate, he detests; and when we earnestly come to Him for help, Satan's host is alarmed. It serves his purpose well if we neglect the exercise of prayer, for then his lying wonders are more readily received" (*Testimonies for the Church,* vol. 1, p. 296.

"An appeal to heaven by the humblest saint is more to be dreaded by Satan than the decrees of cabinets or the mandates of kings" (*S.D.A. Bible Commentary*, vol. 2, p. 1008; *The Signs of the Times*, Oct. 27, 1881).

- *Chapter Sixty-four* -

# It Is Time to Pray

***What a wonder***—"If the Saviour of men, the Son of God, felt the need of prayer, how much more should feeble, sinful mortals feel the necessity of fervent, constant prayer.

"Our heavenly Father waits to bestow upon us the fullness of His blessing. It is our privilege to drink largely at the fountain of boundless love. What a wonder it is that we pray so little! God is ready and willing to hear the sincere prayer of the humblest of His children, and yet there is much manifest reluctance on our part to make known our wants to God" (*Steps to Christ*, p. 94).

***We do not half***—"Look unto Jesus in simplicity and faith. Gaze upon Jesus until the spirit faints under the excess of light. We do not half pray. We do not half believe. 'Ask, and it shall be given you.' Luke 11:9. Pray, believe, strengthen one another. Pray as you never before prayed that the Lord will lay His hand upon you, that you may be able to comprehend the length and breadth and depth and height, and to know the love of Christ, which passeth knowledge, that you may be filled with all the fullness of God" (*Testimonies for the Church,* vol. 7, p. 214).

***Pray as did the Apostles***—"If we are to learn of Christ, we must pray as the apostles prayed when the Holy Spirit was poured upon them. We need a baptism of the Spirit of God. We are not safe for one hour while we are failing to render obedience to the word of God" (*Fundamentals of Christian Education,* p. 537).

***Angels are amazed***—"What can the angels of heaven think of poor helpless human beings, who are subject to temptation, when God's heart of infinite love yearns toward them, ready to give them more than they can ask or think, and yet they pray so little and have so little faith? The angels love to bow before God; they love to be near Him. They regard communion with God as their highest joy; and yet the children of earth, who need so much the help that God only can give, seem satisfied to walk without the light of His Spirit, the companionship of His presence" (*Steps to Christ,* p. 94).

***Darkness encloses***—"The darkness of the evil one encloses those who neglect to pray. The whispered temptations of the enemy entice them to sin; and it is all because they do not make use of the privileges that God has given them in the divine appointment of prayer. Why should the sons and daughters of God be reluctant to pray, when prayer is the key in the hand of faith to unlock heaven's storehouse, where are treasured the boundless resources of Omnipotence? Without unceasing prayer and diligent watching we are in danger of growing careless and of deviating from the right path. The adversary seeks continually to obstruct the way to the mercy seat, that we may not by earnest supplication and faith obtain grace and power to resist temptation" (*Steps to Christ,* pp. 94, 95).

***Pray and labor***—"You may have a deep and abiding sense of eternal things and that love for humanity which Christ has shown in His life. A close connection with Heaven will give the right tone to your fidelity and will be the ground of your success. Your feeling of dependence will drive you to prayer and your sense of duty summon you to effort. Prayer and effort, effort and prayer, will be the business of your life. You must pray as though the efficiency and praise were all due to God, and labor as though duty were all your own. If you want power you may have it, as it is awaiting your draft upon it. Only believe in God, take Him at His word, act by faith, and blessings will come" (*Counsels on Health,* p. 367).

***As though this were your last***—"We must today praise and honor God. By the exercise of living faith today we are to conquer the enemy. We must today seek God and be determined that we will not rest satisfied without His presence. We should watch and work and pray as though this were the last day that would be granted us. How intensely earnest, then, would be our life. How closely would we follow Jesus in all our words and deeds" (*Testimonies for the Church,* vol. 5, p. 200).

*As you have never prayed before*—"There is great necessity for close self-examination in the light of God's word; let each one raise the inquiry: 'Am I sound, or am I rotten at heart? Am I renewed in Christ, or am I still carnal at heart, with a new dress put on the outside?' Rein yourself up to the great tribunal, and in the light of God examine to see if there be any secret sin that you are cherishing, any idol that you have not sacrificed. Pray, yes, pray as you have never prayed before, that you may not be deluded by Satan's devices, that you may not be given up to a heedless, careless, vain spirit, and attend to religious duties to quiet your own conscience" (*Testimonies for the Church,* vol. 2, p. 144).

*Before you speak*—"When about to speak passionately, close your mouth. Don't utter a word. Pray before you speak, and heavenly angels will come to your assistance and drive back the evil angels, who would lead you to dishonor God, reproach His cause, and weaken your own soul" (*Testimonies for the Church,* vol. 2, p. 82).

*Plead the atoning sacrifice*—"Those who look within for comfort will become weary and disappointed. A sense of our weakness and unworthiness should lead us with humility of heart to plead the atoning sacrifice of Christ. As we rely upon His merits we shall find rest and peace and joy. He saves to the uttermost all who come unto God by Him.

"We need to trust in Jesus daily, hourly. He has promised that as our day is, our strength shall be. By His grace we may bear all the burdens of the present and perform its duties. But many are weighed down by the anticipation of future troubles. They are constantly seeking to bring tomorrow's burdens into today. Thus a large share of all their trials are imaginary. For these, Jesus has made no provision. He promises grace only for the day. He bids us not to burden ourselves with the cares and troubles of tomorrow; for 'sufficient unto the day is the evil thereof'" (*Testimonies for the Church,* vol. 5, p. 200).

*Pray in faith—that works*—"Pray in faith. And be sure to bring your lives into harmony with your petitions, that you may receive the blessings for which you pray. Let not your faith weaken, for the blessings received are proportionate to the faith exercised. 'According to your faith be it unto you.' 'All things, whatsoever ye shall ask in prayer, believing, ye shall receive.' Matthew 9:29; 21:22. Pray, believe, rejoice. Sing praises to God because He has answered your prayers. Take Him at His word. 'He is faithful that promised.' Hebrews 10:23. Not one sincere supplication is lost. The channel is open; the stream is flowing. It carries with it healing properties, pouring forth a restoring current of life and health and salvation" (*Testimonies for the Church,* vol. 7, p. 274).

***Pray for loyalty to His law***—"Let no one yield to temptation and become less fervent in his attachment to God's law because of the contempt placed upon it; for that is the very thing that should make us pray with all our heart and soul and voice, 'It is time for thee, Lord, to work: for they have made void thy law.' Therefore, because of the universal contempt, I will not turn traitor when God will be most glorified and most honored by my loyalty....

"When the law of God is most derided and brought into the most contempt, then it is time for every true follower of Christ, for those whose hearts have been given to God, and who are fixed to obey God, to stand unflinchingly for the faith once delivered to the saints. 'Then shall ye return, and discern between the righteous and the wicked, between him that serveth God and him that serveth him not.' It is time to fight when champions are most needed" (*S.D.A. Bible Commentary*, vol. 7, pp. 981, 982).

***Pray when faint-hearted***—"In your business, in companionship for leisure hours, and in alliance for life, let all the associations you form be entered upon with earnest, humble prayer. You will thus show that you honor God, and God will honor you. Pray when you are fainthearted. When you are desponding, close the lips firmly to men; do not shadow the path of others; but tell everything to Jesus. Reach up your hands for help. In your weakness lay hold of infinite strength. Ask for humility, wisdom, courage, increase of faith, that you may see light in God's light and rejoice in His love" (*The Ministry of Healing,* p. 513).

***It is easier to talk***—"It is easier for many to talk than to pray; such lack spirituality and holiness, and their influence is an injury to the cause of God" (*Testimonies for the Church,* vol. 1, pp. 527, 528).

***But do more than pray***—"God does not mean that any of us should become hermits or monks and retire from the world in order to devote ourselves to acts of worship. The life must be like Christ's life between the mountain and the multitude. He who does nothing but pray will soon cease to pray, or his prayers will become a formal routine. When men take themselves out of social life, away from the sphere of Christian duty and cross bearing; when they cease to work earnestly for the Master, who worked earnestly for them, they lose the subject matter of prayer and have no incentive to devotion. Their prayers become personal and selfish. They cannot pray in regard to the wants of humanity or the upbuilding of Christ's kingdom, pleading for strength wherewith to work" (*Steps to Christ,* p. 101).

# Chapter Sixty-five

# *Praying for Our Children*

*A solemn work*—"God sees all the possibilities in that mite of humanity. He sees that with proper training the child will become a power for good in the world. He watches with anxious interest to see whether the parents will carry out His plan or whether by mistaken kindness they will destroy His purpose, indulging the child to its present and eternal ruin. To transform this helpless and apparently insignificant being into a blessing to the world and an honor to God is a great and grand work. Parents should allow nothing to come between them and the obligation they owe to their children" (*The Adventist Home,* p. 264).

*Pray and train*—"In every Christian home God should be honored by the morning and evening sacrifices of prayer and praise. Children should be taught to respect and reverence the hour of prayer. It is the duty of Christian parents, morning and evening, by earnest prayer and persevering faith, to make a hedge about their children.

"In the church at home the children are to learn to pray and to trust in God. Teach them to repeat God's law. Concerning the commandments the Israelites were instructed: 'Thou shalt teach them diligently unto thy children, and shalt talk of them when thou sittest in thine house, and when thou walkest by the way, and when thou liest down, and when thou risest up.' Deuteronomy 6:7. Come in humility, with a heart full of tenderness, and with a sense of the temptations and dangers before yourselves and your children; by faith bind them to the altar, entreating for them the care of the Lord. Train the children to offer their simple words of prayer. Tell them that God delights to have them call upon Him.

"Will the Lord of heaven pass by such homes and leave no blessing there? Nay, verily. Ministering angels will guard the children who are thus dedicated to God. They hear the offering of praise and the prayer of faith, and they bear the petitions of Him who ministers in the sanctuary for His people and offers His merits in their behalf" (*Counsels to Parents, Teachers, and Students*, p. 110).

*He hears and will help*—"You cannot bring up your children as you should without divine help; for the fallen nature of Adam always strives for the mastery. The heart must be prepared for the principles of truth, that they may root in the soul and find nourishment in the life.

"Parents may understand that as they follow God's directions in the training of their children, they will receive help from on high. They receive much benefit; for as they teach, they learn. Their children will achieve victories through the knowledge that they have acquired in keeping the way of the Lord. They are enabled to overcome natural and hereditary tendencies to evil.

"Parents, are you working with unflagging energy in behalf of your children? The God of heaven marks your solicitude, your earnest Work, your constant watchfulness. He hears your prayers. With patience and tenderness train your children for the Lord. All heaven is interested in your work....God will unite with you, crowning your efforts with success.

"As you try to make plain the truths of salvation, and point the children to Christ as a personal Saviour, angels will be by your side. The Lord will give to fathers and mothers grace to interest their little ones in the precious story of the the Babe of Bethlehem, who is indeed the hope of the world" (*The Adventist Home*, pp. 205, 206).

***Eternal consequences are involved***—"You have brought children into the world who have had no voice in regard to their existence. You have made yourselves responsible in a great measure for their future happiness, their eternal well-being. The burden is upon you, whether you are sensible of it or not, to train these children for God, to watch with jealous care the first approach of the wily foe and be prepared to raise a standard against him. Build a fortification of prayer and faith about your children, and exercise diligent watching thereunto. You are not secure a moment against the attacks of Satan. You have no time to rest from watchful, earnest labor. You should not sleep a moment at your post. This is a most important warfare. Eternal consequences are involved. It is life or death with you and your family. Your only safety is to break your hearts before God and seek the kingdom of heaven as little children" (*Testimonies for the Church*, vol. 2, pp. 397, 398).

***Cooperating with God***—"Without human effort divine effort is in vain. God will work with power when in trustful dependence upon Him parents will awake to the sacred responsibility resting upon them and seek to train their children aright. He will cooperate with those parents who carefully and prayerfully educate their children, working out their own and their children's salvation. He will work in them to will and to do of His own good pleasure" (*The Adventist Home,* pp. 206, 207).

***Constantly pray***—"Patiently, lovingly, as faithful stewards of the manifold grace of Christ, parents are to do their appointed work. It is expected of them that they will be found faithful. Everything is to be done in faith. Constantly they must pray that God will impart His grace to their children. Never must they become weary, inpatient, or fretful in their work. They must cling closely to their children and to God. If parents work in patience and love, earnestly endeavoring to help their children to reach the highest standard of purity and modesty, they will succeed" (*The Adventist Home,* p. 208).

"With joy unutterable, parents see the crown, the robe, the harp, given to their children....The seed sown with tears and prayers may have seemed to be sown in vain, but their harvest is reaped with joy at last. Their children have been redeemed" (*Child Guidance*, p. 569).

*A call to pray*—"If ever there was a time when every house should be a house of prayer it is now" (*Testimonies for the Church,* vol. 7, p. 42).

"By sincere, earnest prayer parents should make a hedge about their children. They should pray with full faith that God will abide with them, and that holy angels will guard them and their children from Satan's cruel power" (*Testimonies for the Church,* vol. 7, pp. 42, 43).

"Let parents seek God for guidance in their work. On their knees before Him they will gain a true understanding of their great responsibilities and there they can commit their children to One who will never err in counsel and instruction" (*The Adventist Home,* p. 321).

- Chapter Sixty-six -

# Mother's Prayer

*Moving the arm*—"Those who keep the law of God look upon their children with indefinable feelings of hope and fear, wondering what part they will act in the great conflict that is just before them. The anxious mother questions, 'What stand will they take? What can I do to prepare them to act well their part, so that they will be the recipients of eternal glory?' Great responsibilities rest upon you, mothers. Although you may not stand in national councils,...you may do a great work for God and your country. You may educate your children. You may aid them to develop characters that will not be swayed or influenced to do evil, but will sway and influence others to do right. By your fervent prayers of faith you can move the arm that moves the world" (*The Adventist Home,* p. 264).

*Be much in secret prayer*—"Did mothers but realize the importance of their mission, they would be much in secret prayer, presenting their children to Jesus, imploring His blessing upon them, and pleading for wisdom to discharge aright their sacred duties. Let the mother improve every opportunity to mold and fashion the disposition and habits of her children. Let her watch carefully the development of character, repressing traits that are too prominent, encouraging those that are deficient.

Let her make her own life a pure and noble example to her precious charge.

"The mother should enter upon her work with courage and energy, relying constantly upon divine aid in all her efforts. She should never rest satisfied until she sees in her children a gradual elevation of character, until they have a higher object in life than merely to seek their own pleasure" (*The Adventist Home,* pp. 265, 266).

**When tempted to be irritable**—"But frequently the patience of the mother is taxed with these numerous little trials that seem scarcely worth attention. Mischievous hands and restless feet create a great amount of labor and perplexity for the mother. She has to hold fast the reins of self-control, or impatient words will slip from her tongue. She almost forgets herself time and again, but a silent prayer to her pitying Redeemer calms her nerves, and she is enabled to hold the reins of self-control with quiet dignity. She speaks with calm voice, but it has cost her an effort to restrain harsh words and subdue angry feelings which, if expressed, would have destroyed her influence, which it would have taken time to regain" (*The Adventist Home,* p. 242).

**Heaven is open to every mother's prayers**—"When Christ bowed on the banks of Jordan after His baptism and offered up prayer in behalf of humanity, the heavens were opened; and the Spirit of God, like a dove of burnished gold, encircled the form of the Saviour; and a voice came from heaven which said, 'This is My beloved Son, in whom I am well pleased.'"What significance does this have for you? It says that heaven is open to your prayers. It says that you are accepted in the Beloved. The gates are open for every mother who would lay her burden at the Saviour's feet. It says that Christ has encircled the race with His human arm, and with His divine arm He has grasped the throne of the Infinite and united man with God, and earth with heaven" (*Child Guidance*, pp. 525, 526).

**A precious privilege**—"This is an encouraging lesson to mothers for all time. After they have done the best they can do for the good of their children, they may bring them to Jesus. Even the babes in the mother's arms are precious in His sight. And as the mother's heart yearns for the help she knows she cannot give, the grace she cannot bestow, and she casts herself and children into the merciful arms of Christ, He will receive and bless them; He will give peace, hope, and happiness to mother and children. This is a precious privilege which Jesus has granted to all mothers" (*The Adventist Home,* p. 274).

**Christian mothers' prayers will bear fruit**—"The prayers of Christian mothers are not disregarded by the Father of all....He will not turn away your petitions and leave you and yours to the buffetings of Satan in the great day of final conflict. It is for you to work with simplicity and faithfulness, and God will establish the work of your hands" (*Child Guidance*, p. 526).

"The lifework performed on earth is acknowledged in the heavenly courts as a work well done" (*Child Guidance*, p. 569).

**Influence lasts forever**—"The influence of a praying, God-fearing mother will last through eternity. She may die, but her work will endure" (*Testimonies for the Church,* vol. 4, p. 500).

*- Chapter Sixty-seven -*

# Beware of the Counterfeit

**For every blessing Satan has a counterfeit**—"Whenever and wherever the Lord works in giving a genuine blessing, a counterfeit is also revealed, in order to make of none effect the true work of God" (*Selected Messages,* book 1, p. 142).

**Experience of those who rejected light given in 1844**—"I saw them look up to the throne, and pray, 'Father, give us Thy Spirit.' Satan would then breathe upon them an unholy influence; in it. there was light and much power, but no sweet love, joy and peace. Satan's object was to keep them deceived and to draw back and deceive God's children" (*Early Writings*, p.56).

**In the time of great revival Satan will introduce a counterfeit**—"Before the final visitation of God's judgments upon the earth there will be among the people of the Lord such a revival of primitive godliness as has not been witnessed since apostolic times. The Spirit and power of God will be poured out upon His children....The enemy of souls desires to hinder this work; and before the time for such a movement shall come, he will endeavor to prevent it by introducing a counterfeit. In those churches which he can bring under his deceptive power he will make it appear that God's special blessing is poured out; there will be manifest what is thought to be great religious interest. Multitudes will exult that God is working marvelously for them, when the work is that of another spirit. Under a religious guise, Satan will seek to extend his influence over the Christian world" (*The Great Controversy,* p. 464).

**Satan gives an experience to those who pray while unwilling to obey God**—"In the face of the most positive commands of God, men and women will follow their own inclinations and then dare to pray over the matter, to prevail upon God to consent to allow them to go contrary to His expressed will. The Lord is not pleased with such prayers. Satan comes to the side of such persons, as he did to Eve in Eden, and impresses them, and they have an exercise of mind, and this they relate as a most wonderful experience which the Lord has given them. A true experience will be in perfect harmony with natural and divine law" (*Testimonies for the Church,* vol. 3, pp. 72, 73).

**Our need**—"Every phase of fanaticism and erroneous theories claiming to be the truth, will be brought in among the remnant people of God" (*Selected Messages,* book 2, p. 14).

"We must have our discernment sharpened by divine enlightenment, that we may know the spirit that is of God....Unless we are constantly on guard, we shall be overcome by the enemy" (*Selected Messages,* book 2, pp. 14, 15).

"If we build ourselves up in the faith, we shall be safe in the keeping of the Mighty One" (*Testimonies for the Church,* vol. 5, p. 297).

*- Chapter Sixty-eight -*

# Faith the Key to Answered Prayer

**Faith and prayer**—"I have frequently seen that the children of the Lord neglect prayer, especially secret prayer, altogether too much; that many do not exercise that faith which it is their privilege and duty to exercise, often waiting for that feeling which faith alone can bring. Feeling is not faith; the two are distinct. Faith is ours to exercise, but joyful feeling and the blessing are God's to give. The grace of God comes to the soul through the channel of living faith, and that faith it is in our power to exercise" (*Early Writings,* p. 72).

**Our part: pray and believe**—"Our part is to pray and believe. Watch unto prayer. Watch, and cooperate with the prayer-hearing God. Bear in mind that 'we are labourers together with God.' 1 Corinthians 3:9. Speak and act in harmony with your prayers. It will make an infinite difference with you whether trial shall prove your faith to be genuine, or show that your prayers are only a form.

"When perplexities arise, and difficulties confront you, look not for help to humanity. Trust all with God. The practice of telling our difficulties to others only makes us weak, and brings no strength to them. It lays upon them the burden of our spiritual infirmities, which they cannot relieve. We seek the strength of erring, finite man, when we might have the strength of the unerring, infinite God.

"You need not go to the ends of the earth for wisdom, for God is near. It is not the capabilities you now possess or ever will have that will give you success. It is that which the Lord can do for you. We need to have far less confidence in what man can do and far more confidence in what God can do for every believing soul. He longs to have you reach after Him by faith. He longs to have you expect great things from Him. He longs to give you understanding in temporal as well as in spiritual matters. He can sharpen the intellect. He can give tact and skill. Put your talents into the work, ask God for wisdom, and it will be given you" (*Christ's Object Lessons*, p. 146).

*What no power on earth can do*—"We, too, must have times set apart for meditation and prayer and for receiving spiritual refreshing. We do not value the power and efficacy of prayer as we should. Prayer and faith will do what no power on earth can accomplish. We are seldom, in all respects, placed in the same position twice. We continually have new scenes and new trials to pass through, where past experience cannot be a sufficient guide. We must have the continual light that comes from God" (*The Ministry of Healing*, p. 509).

*Do wonderful things*—"I fear that there is not that faith that is essential. Shall we not brace ourselves against disappointments and temptations to be discouraged? God is merciful, and with the truth rejoicing, purifying, ennobling the life, we can do a sound and solid work for God. Prayer and faith will do wonderful things. The Word must be our weapon of warfare. Miracles can be wrought through the Word; for it is profitable for all things" (*Evangelism*, p. 489).

*The spiritual hand*—"Faith is the spiritual hand that touches infinity" (*Testimonies for the Church*, vol. 6, p. 467).

*Two arms*—"True faith and true prayer how strong they are! They are as two arms by which the human suppliant lays hold upon the power of Infinite Love" (*Gospel Workers*, p. 259).

*Not our Saviour*—"Through faith we receive the grace of God; but faith is not our Saviour. It earns nothing. It is the hand by which we lay hold upon Christ, and appropriate His merits, the remedy for sin" (*The Desire of Ages*, p. 175).

*God reaches for our hand*—"God reaches for the hand of faith in us to direct it to lay fast hold upon the divinity of Christ, that we may attain to perfection of character" (*The Desire of Ages*, p. 123).

***Faith see Jesus as our Mediator***—"Faith sees Jesus standing as our Mediator at the right hand of God" (*Gospel Workers,* p. 259).

"Today He is standing at the altar of mercy, presenting before God the prayers of those who desire His help" (*The Ministry of Healing,* p. 90).

"As the sinner's sincere, humble prayers ascend to the throne of God, Christ mingles with them the merits of His own life of perfect obedience. Our prayers are made fragrant by this incense. Christ has pledged Himself to intercede in our behalf, and the Father always hears the Son" (*Sons and Daughters of God,* p. 22).

***The prayer of faith defined***—"The prayer that comes from an earnest heart, when the simple wants of the soul are expressed just as we would ask an earthly friend for a favor, expecting that it would be granted this is the prayer of faith" (*My Life Today,* p. 19).

***The foundation of genuine faith***—"Genuine faith has its foundation in the promises and provisions of the Scriptures" (*Gospel Workers,* p. 260).

"We are not to trust in our faith, but in the promises of God" (*Messages to Young People*, p. 111).

***Brings the richest blessings***—"We do not enjoy the fullness of blessing which the Lord has prepared for us, because we do not ask in faith. If we would exercise faith in the word of the living God we should have the richest blessings. We dishonor God by our lack of faith; therefore we cannot impart life to others by bearing a living, uplifting testimony. We cannot give that which we do not possess" (*Testimonies for the Church*, vol. 6, p. 63).

***For the disheartened***—"For all who are disheartened there is but one remedy, faith, prayer and work" (*Testimonies for the Church*, vol. 6, p. 438).

***Must not let go***—"Your faith must not let go of the promises of God, if you do not see or feel the immediate answer to your prayers. Be not afraid to trust God. Rely upon His sure promise: 'Ask, and ye shall receive.' God is too wise to err, and too good to withhold any good thing from His saints that walk uprightly" (*Testimonies for the Church,* vol. 1, p. 120).

***Faith strengthened by prayer***—"Instead of strengthening their faith by prayer and meditation on the words of Christ, they had been dwelling on their discouragements and personal grievances. In this state of darkness they had undertaken the conflict with Satan.

"In order to succeed in such a conflict they must come to the work in a different spirit. Their faith must be strengthened by fervent prayer and fasting, and humiliation of heart. They must be emptied of self, and be filled with the Spirit and power of God. Earnest, persevering supplication to God in faith faith that leads to entire dependence upon God, and unreserved consecration to His work can alone avail to bring men the Holy Spirit's aid in the battle against principalities and powers, the rulers of the darkness of this world, and wicked spirits in high places" (*The Desire of Ages,* p. 431).

*Victory every day*—"The people of God must move understandingly. They should not be satisfied until every known sin is confessed; then it is their privilege and duty to believe that Jesus accepts them. They must not wait for others to press through the darkness and obtain the victory for them to enjoy. Such enjoyment will last only till the meeting closes. But God must be served from principle instead of from feeling. Morning and night obtain the victory for yourselves in your own family. Let not your daily labor keep you from this. Take time to pray, and as you pray, believe that God hears you. Have faith mixed with your prayers. You may not at all times feel the immediate answer; but then it is that faith is tried. You are proved to see whether you will trust in God, whether you have living, abiding faith. 'Faithful is He that calleth you, who also will do it.' Walk the narrow plank of faith. Trust all on the promises of the Lord. Trust God in darkness. That is the time to have faith. But you often let feeling govern you. You look for worthiness in yourselves when you do not feel comforted by the Spirit of God, and despair because you cannot find it. You do not trust enough to Jesus, precious Jesus. You do not make His worthiness to be all, all. The very best you can do will not merit the favor of God. It is Jesus' worthiness that will save you, His blood that will cleanse you. But you have efforts to make. You must do what you can do on your part. Be zealous and repent, then believe.

"Confound not faith and feeling together. They are distinct. Faith is ours to exercise. This faith we must keep in exercise. Believe, believe. Let your faith take hold of the blessing, and it is yours. Your feelings have nothing to do with this faith. When faith brings the blessing to your heart, and you rejoice in the blessing, it is no more faith, but feeling" (*Testimonies for the Church,* vol. 1, p. 167).

*Look, O look!*—"One who knows, has said, 'The Father Himself loveth you.' One who has had an experimental knowledge of the length, and breadth, and height, and depth of that love, has declared unto us this amazing fact. This love is ours through faith in the Son of God, therefore a connection with Christ means everything to us. We are to be one with Him as He is one with the Father, and then we are beloved by the infinite God as members of the body of Christ, as branches of the living Vine. We are to be attached to the parent stock, and to receive nourishment from the Vine. Christ is our glorified Head, and the divine love flowing from the heart of God, rests in Christ, and is communicated to those who have been united to Him. This divine love entering the soul inspires it with gratitude, frees it from its spiritual feebleness, from pride, vanity, and selfishness, and from all that would deform the Christian character....

"When we seek for appropriate language in which to describe the love of God, we find words too tame, too weak, too far beneath the theme, and we lay down our pen and say, 'No, it cannot be described.' We can only do as did the beloved disciple, and say, 'Behold, what manner of love the Father hath bestowed upon us, that we should be called the sons of God.' In attempting any description of this love, we feel that we are as infants lisping their first words. Silently we may adore; for silence in this matter is the only eloquence. This love is past all language to describe. It is the mystery of God in the flesh, God in Christ, and divinity in humanity. Christ bowed down in unparalleled humility, that in His exaltation to the throne of God, He might also exalt those who believe in Him, to a seat with Him upon His throne. All who look upon Jesus in faith that the wounds and bruises that sin has made will be healed in Him, shall be made whole.

"The themes of redemption are momentous themes, and only those who are spiritually minded can discern their depth and significance. It is our safety, our life, our joy, to dwell upon the truths of the plan of salvation. Faith and prayer are necessary in order that we may behold the deep things of God" (*Fundamentals of Christian Education*, pp. 178-180).

- Chapter Sixty-nine -

# God Invites You to Come

*A special invitation*—"We come to God by special invitation, and He waits to welcome us to His audience chamber....Let those who desire the blessing of God knock and wait at the door of mercy with firm assurance, saying, For Thou, O Lord, hast said, 'Everyone that asketh receiveth; and he that seeketh findeth; and to him that knocketh it shall be opened'" (*Thoughts from the Mount of Blessing,* p. 131).

*Ask help for every need*—"We may tell the Lord, with the simplicity of a child, exactly what we need. We may state to Him our temporal matters, asking Him for bread and raiment as well as for the bread of life and the robe of Christ's righteousness. Your heavenly Father knows that you have need of all these things, and you are invited to ask Him concerning them. It is through the name of Jesus that every favor is received. God will honor that name, and will supply your necessities from the riches of His liberality" (*Thoughts from the Mount of Blessing,* p. 133).

*Gifts so precious*—"The gifts of Him who has all power in heaven and earth are in store for the children of God. Gifts so precious that they come to us through the costly sacrifice of the Redeemer's blood; gifts that will satisfy the deepest craving of the heart, gifts lasting as eternity, will be received and enjoyed by all who will come to God as little children" (*Thoughts from the Mount of Blessing*, pp. 133, 134).

*Temporal and spiritual blessings*—"He longs to give you understanding in temporal as well as in spiritual matters. He can sharpen the intellect. He can give tact and skill. Put your talents into the work, ask God for wisdom, and it will be given you" (*Christ's Object Lessons*, p. 146).

*Whatever your problems*—" 'Come unto Me,' is His invitation. Whatever your anxieties and trials, spread out your case before the Lord" (*The Desire of Ages*, p. 329).

*Come now, boldly*—"Heaven is open to our petitions, and we are invited to come 'boldly unto the throne of grace, that we may obtain mercy, and find grace to help in time of need.' We are to come in faith, believing that we shall obtain the very things we ask of Him" (*S.D.A. Bible Commentary*, vol. 5, p. 1078; *The Signs of the Times*, April 18, 1892).

- Chapter Seventy -

# How Enoch Prayed

*Silent petitions while in daily work*—"While engaged in our daily work, we should lift the soul to heaven in prayer. These silent petitions rise like incense before the throne of grace; and the enemy is baffled....It was thus that Enoch walked with God. And God was with him, a present help in every time of need....

"Prayer is the breath of the soul. It is the secret of spiritual power. No other means of grace can be substituted, and the health of the soul be preserved. Prayer brings the heart into immediate contact with the Wellspring of life, and strengthens the sinew and muscle of the religious experience" (*Gospel Workers*, pp. 254, 255).

*Unceasing prayer*—"I wish I could impress upon every worker in God's cause the great need of continual, earnest prayer. They cannot be constantly upon their knees, but they can be lifting their hearts to God. This the way that Enoch walked with God" (*Testimonies for the Church*, vol. 5, p. 596).

"Enoch's walk with God was not in a trance or a vision, but in all the duties of his daily life....In the family and in his intercourse with men, as a husband and father, a friend, a citizen, he was the steadfast, unwavering servant of the Lord" (*Patriarchs and Prophets*, p. 85).

*Type of remnant*—"The godly character of this prophet represents the state of holiness which must be attained by those who shall be 'redeemed from the earth' (Revelation 14:3) at the time of Christ's second advent....Like Enoch, God's people will seek for purity of heart, and conformity to His will, until they shall reflect the likeness of Christ. Like Enoch...by their holy conversation and example they will condemn the sins of the ungodly. As Enoch was translated to heaven before the destruction of the world by water, so the living righteous will be translated from the earth before its destruction by fire" (*Patriarchs and Prophets*, pp. 88, 89).

*Lived in heavenly places*—"Enoch's heart was upon eternal treasures. He had looked upon the celestial city. He had seen the King in His glory in the midst of Zion. The greater the existing iniquity, the more earnest was his longing for the home of God....

"'Blessed are the pure in heart; for they shall see God.' For three hundred years Enoch had been seeking purity of heart, that he might be in harmony with heaven. For three centuries he had walked with God. Day by day he had longed for a closer union; nearer and nearer had grown the communion, until God took him to Himself. He had stood at the threshold of the eternal world, only a step between him and the land of the blest; and now the portals opened, the walk with God, so long pursued on earth, continued, and he passed through the gates of the Holy City....

"To such communion God is calling us" (*Testimonies for the Church*, vol. 8, pp. 330, 331).

- *Chapter Seventy-one* -

# How Moses Prayed

*Tell Him your problems*—"The Lord has given us the promise, 'If any of you lack wisdom, let him ask of God, that giveth to all men liberally, and upbraideth not; and it shall be given him.' It is in the order of God that those who bear responsibilities should often meet together to counsel with one another, and to pray earnestly for that wisdom which He alone can impart. Talk less; much precious time is lost in talk that brings no light. Let brethren unite in fasting and prayer for the wisdom that God has promised to supply liberally. Make known your troubles to God. Tell Him, as did Moses, 'I cannot lead this people unless Thy presence shall go with me.' And then ask still more; pray with Moses, 'Show me Thy glory.' What is this glory? The character of God. This is what He proclaimed to Moses.

"Let the soul in living faith fasten upon God. Let the tongue speak His praise. When you associate together, let the mind be reverently turned to the contemplation of eternal realities. Thus you will be helping one another to be spiritually minded. When your will is in harmony with the divine will, you will be in harmony with one another; you will have Christ by your side as a counselor" (*Gospel Workers,* p. 417).

***Pleading for His people***—"'Let me alone,…that I may consume them,' were the words of God. If God had purposed to destroy Israel, who could plead for them? How few but would have left the sinners to their fate!…

"But Moses discerned ground for hope where there appeared only discouragement and wrath. The words of God, 'Let Me alone,' he understood not to forbid but to encourage intercession, implying that nothing but the prayers of Moses could save Israel.…

"As Moses interceded for Israel, his timidity was lost in his deep interest and love for those for whom he had, in the hands of God, been the means of doing so much. The Lord listened to his pleadings, and granted his unselfish prayer. God had proved His servant; He had tested his faithfulness and his love for that erring, ungrateful people, and nobly had Moses endured the trial. His interest in Israel sprang from no selfish motive. The prosperity of God's chosen people was dearer to him than personal honor, dearer than the privilege of becoming the father of a mighty nation" (*Patriarchs and Prophets*, pp. 318, 319; also *Testimonies for the Church*, vol. 3, pp. 297, 298).

***He must have help from God***—"Moses knew well the perversity and blindness of those who were placed under his care; he knew the difficulties with which he must contend. But he had learned that in order to prevail with the people, he must have help from God. He pleaded for a clearer revelation of God's will and for an assurance of His presence: 'See, Thou sayest unto me, Bring up this people: and Thou hast not let me know whom Thou wilt send with me. Yet Thou hast said, I know thee by name, and thou hast also found grace in My sight. Now therefore, I pray Thee, if I have found grace in Thy sight, show me now Thy way, that I may know Thee, that I may find grace in Thy sight; and consider that this nation is Thy people.'

"The answer was, 'My presence shall go with thee, and I will give thee rest.' But Moses was not yet satisfied. There pressed upon his soul a sense of the terrible results should God leave Israel to hardness and impenitence. He could not endure that his interests should be separated from those of his brethren, and he prayed that the favor of

God might be restored to His people, and that the token of His presence might continue to direct their journeyings: 'If Thy presence go not with me, carry us not up hence. For wherein shall it be known here that I and Thy people have found grace in Thy sight? is it not in that Thou goest with us? So shall we be separated, I and Thy people, from all the people that are upon the face of the earth.'

"And the Lord said, 'I will do this thing also that thou hast spoken: for thou hast found grace in My sight, and I know thee by name.' Still the prophet did not cease pleading. Every prayer had been answered, but he thirsted for greater tokens of God's favor. He now made a request that no human being had ever made before: 'I beseech Thee, show me Thy glory.'

"God did not rebuke his request as presumptuous; but the gracious words were spoken, 'I will make all My goodness pass before thee.' The unveiled glory of God, no man in this mortal state can look upon and live; but Moses was assured that he should behold as much of divine glory as he could endure. Again he was summoned to the mountain summit; then the hand that made the world, that hand that 'removeth the mountains, and they know not' (Job 9:5), took this creature of the dust, this mighty man of faith, and placed him in a cleft of the rock, while the glory of God and all His goodness passed before him.

"This experience, above all else the promise that the divine Presence would attend him, was to Moses an assurance of success in the work before him; and he counted it of infinitely greater worth than all the learning of Egypt or all his attainments as a statesman or a military leader. No earthly power or skill or learning can supply the place of God's abiding presence" (*Patriarchs and Prophets*, pp. 327, 328; also *Testimonies for the Church*, vol. 4, pp. 532, 533).

*More pleading for the church*—"The heart of Moses sank. He had pleaded that Israel should not be destroyed, even though his own posterity might then become a great nation. In his love for them he had prayed that his name might be blotted from the book of life rather than that they should be left to perish. He had imperiled all for them, and this was their response. All their hardships, even their imaginary sufferings, they charged upon him; and their wicked murmurings made doubly heavy the burden of care and responsibility under which he staggered" (*Patriarchs and Prophets*, pp. 379, 380).

*Still more pleading for the disobedient*—"Moses now arose and entered the tabernacle. The Lord declared to him, 'I will smite them with the pestilence, and disinherit them, and will make of thee a greater nation.' But again Moses pleaded for his people. He could not consent to have them destroyed, and he himself made a mightier nation. Appealing to the mercy of God, he said: 'I beseech Thee, let the power of my Lord be great according as Thou hast spoken, saying, The Lord is long-suffering, and of great mercy....Pardon, I beseech Thee, the iniquity of this people according to the greatness of Thy mercy, and as Thou hast forgiven this people, from Egypt even until now'" (*Patriarchs and Prophets*, pp. 390, 391).

*Flat on the ground*—"Moses and Aaron still remained prostrate before God in the presence of all the assembly, silently imploring divine mercy for rebellious Israel. Their distress was too deep for words. Again Caleb and Joshua press to the front, and the voice of Caleb once more rises in sorrowful earnestness above the complaints of the congregation: 'The land, which we passed through to search it, is an exceeding good land. If the Lord delight in us, then He will bring us into this land, and give it us; a land which floweth with milk and honey. Only rebel not ye against the Lord, neither fear ye the people of the land; for they are bread for us: their defense is departed from them, and the Lord is with us: fear them not'" (*Patriarchs and Prophets*, p. 151).

*Amid more rebellion*—"Moses had not suspected this deep-laid plot, and when its terrible significance burst upon him, he fell upon his face in silent appeal to God. He arose sorrowful indeed, but calm and strong. Divine guidance had been granted him" (*Patriarchs and Prophets*, p. 398).

*Prostrated before the Lord*—"Here we find a striking exhibition of the blindness that will compass human minds that turn from light and evidence. Here we see the strength of settled rebellion, and how difficult it is to be subdued. Surely the Hebrews had had the most convincing evidence in the destruction of the men who had deceived them; but they still stood forth boldly and defiantly, and accused Moses and Aaron of killing good and holy men. 'For rebellion is as the sin of witchcraft, and stubbornness is as iniquity and idolatry.'

"Moses did not feel the guilt of sin and did not hasten away at the word of the Lord and leave the congregation to perish, as the Hebrews had fled from the tents of Korah, Dathan, and Abiram the day before. Moses lingered; for he could not consent to give up all that vast multitude to perish, although he knew that they deserved the vengeance of God for their persistent rebellion. He prostrated himself before God because the people felt no necessity for humiliation; he mediated for them because they felt no need of interceding in their own behalf" (*Testimonies for the Church,* vol. 3, pp. 357, 358).

*Ready to kill him*—"They were about to proceed to violence against their faithful, self-sacrificing leaders.

"A manifestation of the divine glory was seen in the cloud above the tabernacle, and a voice from the cloud spoke to Moses and Aaron, 'Get you up from among this congregation, that I may consume them as in a moment.'

"The guilt of sin did not rest upon Moses, and hence he did not fear and did not hasten away and leave the congregation to perish. Moses lingered, in this fearful crisis manifesting the true shepherd's interest for the flock of his care. He pleaded that the wrath of God might not utterly destroy the people of His choice. By his intercession he stayed the arm of vengeance, that a full end might not be made of disobedient, rebellious Israel" (*Patriarchs and Prophets*, p. 402).

*Time for parting*—"As the people gazed upon the aged man, so soon to be taken from them, they recalled, with a new and deeper appreciation, his parental tenderness, his wise counsels, and his untiring labors. How often, when their sins had invited the just judgments of God the prayers of Moses had prevailed with Him to spare them! Their grief was heightened by remorse. They bitterly remembered that their own perversity had provoked Moses to the sin for which he must die" (*Patriarchs and Prophets*, p. 470).

*Answered at last*—"Never, till exemplified in the sacrifice of Christ, were the justice and the love of God more strikingly displayed than in His dealings with Moses. God shut Moses out of Canaan, to teach a lesson which should never be forgotten that He requires exact obedience, and that men are to beware of taking to themselves the glory which is due to their Maker. He could not grant the prayer of Moses that he might share the inheritance of Israel, but He did not forget or forsake His servant. The God of heaven understood the suffering that Moses had endured; He had noted every act of faithful service through those long years of conflict and trial. On the top of Pisgah, God called Moses to an inheritance infinitely more glorious than the earthly Canaan.

"Upon the mount of transfiguration Moses was present with Elijah, who had been translated. They were sent as bearers of light and glory from the Father to His Son. And thus the prayer of Moses, uttered so many centuries before, was at last fulfilled. He stood upon the 'goodly mountain,' within the heritage of his people, bearing witness to Him in whom all the promises to Israel centered. Such is the last scene revealed to mortal vision in the history of that man so highly honored of Heaven" (*Patriarchs and Prophets*, p. 479).

*They shared His longing*—"Now heaven had sent its messengers to Jesus; not angels, but men who had endured suffering and sorrow, and who could sympathize with the Saviour in the trial of His earthly life. Moses and Elijah had been co-laborers with Christ. They had shared His longing for the salvation of men. Moses had pleaded for Israel; 'Yet now, if Thou wilt forgive their sin ; and if not, blot me, I pray thee, out of Thy book which Thou hast written.' Exodus 32:32. Elijah had known loneliness of spirit, as for three years and a half of famine he had borne the burden of the nation's hatred and its woe. Alone he had stood for God upon Mount Carmel. Alone he had fled to the desert in anguish and despair. These men, chosen above every angel around the throne, had come to commune with Jesus concerning the scenes of His suffering, and to comfort Him with the assurance of the sympathy of heaven. The hope of the world, the salvation of every human being, was the burden of their interview" (*The Desire of Ages,* pp. 422-425).

*- Chapter Seventy-two -*

# How Elijah Prayed

*As He did then*—"God's messengers must tarry long with Him, if they would have success in their work. The story is told of an old Lancashire woman who was listening to the reasons that her neighbors gave for their minister's success. They spoke of gifts, of his style of address, of his manners. 'Nay,' said the old woman, 'I will tell you what it is. Your man is very thick with the Almighty.'

"When men are as devoted as Elijah was and possess the faith that he had, God will reveal Himself as He did then. When men plead with the Lord as did Jacob, the results that were seen then will again be seen. Power will come from God in answer to the prayer of faith" (*Gospel Workers,* p. 255).

*He prayed because he was concerned*—"Among the mountains of Gilead, east of the Jordan, there dwelt in the days of Ahab a man of faith and prayer whose fearless ministry was destined to check the rapid spread of apostasy in Israel. Far removed from any city of renown, and occupying no high station in life, Elijah the Tishbite nevertheless entered upon his mission confident in God's purpose to prepare the way before him and to give him abundant success. The word of faith and power was upon his lips, and his whole life was devoted to the work of reform. His was the voice of one crying in the wilderness to rebuke sin and press back the tide of evil. And while he came to the people as a reprover of sin, his message offered the balm of Gilead to the sin-sick souls of all who desired to be healed.

"As Elijah saw Israel going deeper and deeper into idolatry, his soul was distressed and his indignation aroused. God had done great things for His people. He had delivered them from bondage and given them 'the lands of the heathen,... that they might observe His statutes, and keep His laws.' Psalm 105: 44, 45. But the beneficent designs of Jehovah were now well-nigh forgotten. Unbelief was fast separating the chosen nation from the Source of their strength. Viewing this apostasy from his mountain retreat, Elijah was overwhelmed with sorrow. In anguish of soul he besought God to arrest the once-favored people in their wicked course, to visit them with judgments, if need be, that they might be led to see in its true light their departure from Heaven. He longed to see them brought to repentance before they should go to such lengths in evil-doing as to provoke the Lord to destroy them utterly.

"Elijah's prayer was answered. Oft-repeated appeals, remonstrances, and warnings had failed to bring Israel to repentance. The time had come when God must speak to them by means of judgments" (*Prophets and Kings,* pp. 119, 120).

***There was one who dared***—"The fear of God was daily growing less in Israel. The blasphemous tokens of their blind idolatry were to be seen among the Israel of God. There were none who dared to expose their lives by openly standing forth in opposition to the prevailing blasphemous idolatry. The altars of Baal, and the priests of Baal who sacrificed to the sun, moon, and stars, were conspicuous everywhere. They had consecrated temples and groves wherein the work of men's hands was placed to be worshiped. The benefits which God gave to this people called forth from them no gratitude to the Giver. All the bounties of heaven, the running brooks, the streams of living waters, the gentle dew, the showers of rain which refreshed the earth and caused their fields to bring forth abundantly, these they ascribed to the favor of their gods.

"Elijah's faithful soul was grieved. His indignation was aroused, and he was jealous for the glory of God. He saw that Israel was 'plunged into fearful apostasy. And when he called to mind the great things that God had wrought for them, he was overwhelmed with grief and amazement. But all this was forgotten by the majority of the people. He went before the Lord, and, with his soul wrung with anguish, pleaded for Him to save His people if it must be by judgments. He pleaded with God to withhold from His ungrateful people dew and rain, the treasures of heaven, that apostate Israel might look in vain to their gods, their idols of gold, wood, and stone, the sun, moon, and stars, to water and enrich the earth, and cause it to bring forth plentifully. The Lord told Elijah that He had heard his prayer and would withhold dew and rain from His people until they should turn unto Him with repentance" (*Testimonies for the Church,* vol. 3, pp. 262, 263).

***He continued those prayers***—"Through the long years of drought and famine, Elijah prayed earnestly that the hearts of Israel might be turned from idolatry to allegiance to God. Patiently the prophet waited, while the hand of the Lord rested heavily on the stricken land. As he saw evidences of suffering and want multiplying on every side, his heart was wrung with sorrow, and he longed for power to bring about a reformation quickly. But God Himself was working out His plan, and all that His servant could do was to pray on in faith and await the time for decided action" (*Prophets and Kings,* p. 133).

*He prays as if he knows*—"Reminding the people of the long-continued apostasy that has awakened the wrath of Jehovah, Elijah calls upon them to humble their hearts and turn to the God of their fathers, that the curse upon the land of Israel may be removed. Then, bowing reverently before the unseen God, he raises his hands toward heaven and offers a simple prayer. Baal's priests have screamed and foamed and leaped, from early morning until late in the afternoon; but as Elijah prays, no senseless shrieks resound over Carmel's height. He prays as if he knows Jehovah is there, a witness to the scene, a listener to his appeal. The prophets of Baal have prayed wildly, incoherently. Elijah prays simply and fervently, asking God to show His superiority over Baal, that Israel may be led to turn to Him.

"'Lord God of Abraham, Isaac, and of Israel,' the prophet pleads, 'let it be known this day that Thou art God in Israel, and that I am Thy servant, and that I have done all these things at Thy word. Hear me, O Lord, hear me, that this people may know that Thou art the Lord God, and that Thou hast turned their heart back again.'

"A silence, oppressive in its solemnity, rests upon all. The priests of Baal tremble with terror. Conscious of their guilt, they look for swift retribution.

"No sooner is the prayer of Elijah ended than flames of fire, like brilliant flashes of lightning, descend from heaven upon the upreared altar, consuming the sacrifice, licking up the water in the trench, and consuming even the stones of the altar. The brilliancy of the blaze illumines the mountain and dazzles the eyes of the multitude. In the valleys below, where many are watching in anxious suspense the movements of those above, the descent of fire is clearly seen, and all are amazed at the sight. It resembles the pillar of fire which at the Red Sea separated the children of Israel from the Egyptian host" (*Prophets and Kings,* pp. 152, 153).

*His face between his knees*—"With the slaying of the prophets of Baal, the way was opened for carrying forward a mighty spiritual reformation among the ten tribes of the northern kingdom. Elijah had set before the people their apostasy; he had called upon them to humble their hearts and turn to the Lord. The judgments of Heaven had been executed; the people had confessed their sins, and had acknowledged the God of their fathers as the living God; and now the curse of Heaven was to be withdrawn, and the temporal blessings of life renewed. The land was to be refreshed with rain. 'Get thee up, eat and drink,' Elijah said to Ahab; 'for there is a sound of abundance of rain.' Then the prophet went to the top of the mount to pray.

"It was not because of any outward evidence that the showers were about to fall, that Elijah could so confidently bid Ahab prepare for rain. The prophet saw no clouds in the heavens; he heard no thunder. He simply spoke the word that the Spirit of the Lord had moved him to speak in response to his own strong faith. Throughout the day he had unflinchingly performed the will of God and had revealed his implicit confidence in the prophecies of God's word; and now, having done all that was in his power to do, he knew that Heaven would freely bestow the blessings foretold. The same God who had sent the drought had promised an abundance of rain as the reward of rightdoing; and now Elijah waited for the promised outpouring. In an attitude of humility, 'his face between his knees,' he interceded with God in behalf of penitent Israel.

"Again and again Elijah sent his servant to a point overlooking the Mediterranean, to learn whether there were any visible token that God had heard his prayer. Each time the servant returned with the word, 'There is nothing.' The prophet did not become impatient or lose faith, but continued his earnest pleading. Six times the servant returned with the word that there was no sign of rain in the brassy heavens. Undaunted, Elijah sent him forth once more; and this time the servant returned with the word, 'Behold, there ariseth a little cloud out of the sea, like a man's hand.'

"This was enough. Elijah did not wait for the heavens to gather blackness. In that small cloud he beheld by faith an abundance of rain; and he acted in harmony with his faith, sending his servant quickly to Ahab with the message, 'Prepare thy chariot, and get thee down, that the rain stop thee not.'

"It was because Elijah was a man of large faith that God could use him in this grave crisis in the history of Israel. As he prayed, his faith reached out and grasped the promises of Heaven, and he persevered in prayer until his petitions were answered. He did not wait for the full evidence that God had heard him, but was willing to venture all on the slightest token of divine favor. And yet what he was enabled to do under God, all may do in their sphere of activity in God's service; for of the prophet from the mountains of Gilead it is written: 'Elias was a man subject to like passions as we are, and he prayed earnestly that it might not rain: and it rained not on the earth by the space of three years and six months.' James 5:17.

"Faith such as this is needed in the world today faith that will lay hold on the promises of God's word and refuse to let go until Heaven hears. Faith such as this connects us closely with Heaven, and brings us strength for coping with the powers of darkness. Through faith God's children have 'subdued kingdoms, wrought righteousness, obtained promises, stopped the mouths of lions, quenched the violence of fire, escaped the edge of the sword, out of weakness were made strong, waxed valiant in fight, turned to flight the armies of the aliens.' Hebrews 11:33, 34. And through faith we today are to reach the heights of God's purpose for us. 'If thou canst believe, all things are possible to him that believeth.' Mark 9:23.

"Faith is an essential element of prevailing prayer. 'He that cometh to God must believe that He is, and that He is a rewarder of them that diligently seek Him.' 'If we ask anything according to His will, He heareth us: and if we know that He hear us, whatsoever we ask, we know that we have the petitions that we desired of Him.' Hebrews 11:6; 1 John 5:14, 15. With the persevering faith of Jacob, with the unyielding persistence of Elijah, we may present our petitions to the Father, claiming all that

He has promised. The honor of His throne is staked for the fulfillment of His word" (*Prophets and Kings,* pp. 155-158).

***Important lessons***—"Important lessons are presented to us in the experience of Elijah. When upon Mt. Carmel he offered the prayer for rain, his faith was tested, but he persevered in making known his request unto God. Six times he prayed earnestly, and yet there was no sign that his petition was granted, but with a strong faith he urged his plea to the throne of grace. Had he given up in discouragement at the sixth time, his prayer would not have been answered, but he persevered till the answer came. We have a God whose ear is not closed to our petitions; and if we prove His word, He will honor our faith. He wants us to have all our interests interwoven with His interests, and then He can safely bless us; for we shall not then take glory to self when the blessing is ours, but shall render all the praise to God. God does not always answer our prayers the first time we call upon Him; for should He do this, we might take it for granted that we had a right to all the blessings and favors He bestowed upon us. Instead of searching our hearts to see if any evil was entertained by us, any sin indulged, we should become careless, and fail to realize our dependence upon Him, and our need of His help.

"Elijah humbled himself until he was in a condition where he would not take the glory to himself. This is the condition upon which the Lord hears prayer, for then we shall give the praise to Him. The custom of offering praise to men is one that results in great evil. One praises another, and thus men are led to feel that glory and honor belong to them. When you exalt man, you lay a snare for his soul, and do just as Satan would have you. You should praise God with all your heart, soul, might, mind, and strength; for God alone is worthy to be glorified" (*S.D.A. Bible Commentary,* vol. 2, pp. 1034, 1035; *The Review and Herald,* Mar. 27, 1913).

***Less and less***—"The servant watched while Elijah prayed....As he searched his heart, he seemed to be less and less, both in his own estimation and in the sight of God. It seemed to him that he was nothing, and that God was everything; and when he reached the point of renouncing self, while he clung to the Saviour as his only strength and righteousness, the answer came" (*Sons and Daughters of God,* p. 206).

***Ye let go too soon***—"We should be much in secret prayer. Christ is the vine, ye are the branches. And if we would grow and flourish, we must continually draw sap and nourishment from the Living Vine; for separated from the Vine we have no strength.

"I asked the angel why there was no more faith and power in Israel. He said, 'Ye let go of the arm of the Lord too soon. Press your petitions to the throne, and hold on by strong faith. The promises are sure. Believe ye receive the things ye ask for, and ye shall have them.' I was then pointed to Elijah. He was subject to like passions as we are, and he prayed earnestly. His faith endured the trial. Seven times he prayed before the Lord, and at last the cloud was seen. I saw that we had doubted the sure promises, and wounded the Saviour by our lack of faith. Said the angel, 'Gird the armor about thee, and above all take the shield of faith; for that will guard the heart, the very life, from the fiery darts of the wicked.' If the enemy can lead the desponding to take their eyes off from Jesus, and look to themselves, and dwell upon their own unworthiness, instead of dwelling upon the worthiness of Jesus, His love, His merits, and His great mercy, he will get away their shield of faith and gain his object; they will be exposed to his fiery temptations. The weak should therefore look to Jesus, and believe in Him; they then exercise faith" (*Early Writings*, p. 73).

- *Chapter Seventy-three* -

# How Hezekiah Prayed

**He laid it before the Lord**—" 'Beware lest Hezekiah persuade you, saying, The Lord will deliver us. Hath any of the gods of the nations delivered his land out of the hand of the king of Assyria? Where are the gods of Hamath and Arphad? where are the gods of Sepharvaim? and have they delivered Samaria out of my hand? Who are they among all the gods of these lands, that have delivered their land out of my hand, that the Lord should deliver Jerusalem out of my hand?' Isaiah 36:13-20....

"Sennacherib wrote 'letters to rail on the Lord God of Israel, and to speak against Him, saying, As the gods of the nations of other lands have not delivered their people out of mine hand, so shall not the God of Hezekiah deliver His people out of mine hand.' 2 Chronicles 32:17.

"The boastful threat was accompanied by the message: 'Let not thy God in whom thou trustest deceive thee, saying, Jerusalem shall not be delivered into the hand of the king of Assyria. Behold, thou hast heard what the kings of Assyria have done to all lands, by destroying them utterly: and shalt thou be delivered? Have the gods of the nations delivered them which my fathers have destroyed; as Gozan, and Haran, and Rezeph, and the children of Eden which were in Thelasar? Where is the king of Hamath, and the king of Arpad, and the king of the city of Sepharvaim, of Hena, and Ivah?' 2 Kings 19:10-13.

"When the king of Judah received the taunting letter, he took it into the temple and 'spread it before the Lord' and prayed with strong faith for help from heaven, that the nations of earth might know that the God of the Hebrews still lived and reigned. Verse 14. The honor of Jehovah was at stake; He alone could bring deliverance.

" 'O Lord God of Israel, which dwellest between the cherubims,' Hezekiah pleaded, 'Thou art the God, even Thou alone, of all the kingdoms of the earth; Thou hast made heaven and earth. Lord, bow down Thine ear, and hear: open, Lord, Thine eyes, and see: and hear the words of Sennacherib, which hath sent him to reproach the living God. Of a truth, Lord, the kings of Assyria have destroyed the nations and their lands, and have cast their gods into the fire: for they were no gods, but the work of men's hands, wood and stone: therefore they have destroyed them. Now therefore, O Lord, our God, I beseech Thee, save Thou us out of his hand, that all the kingdoms of the earth may know that Thou art the Lord God, even Thou only.' 2 Kings 19:15-19....

"Hezekiah's pleadings in behalf of Judah and of the honor of their Supreme Ruler were in harmony with the mind of God. Solomon, in his benediction at the dedication of the temple, had prayed the Lord to maintain 'the cause of His people Israel at all times, as the matter shall require: that all the people of the earth may know that the Lord is God, and that there is none else.' 1 Kings 8:59, 60. Especially was the Lord to show favor when, in times of war or of oppression by an army, the chief men of Israel should enter the house of prayer and plead for deliverance. Verses 33, 34.

"Hezekiah was not left without hope. Isaiah sent to him, saying, 'Thus saith the Lord God of Israel, That which thou hast prayed to Me against Sennacherib king of Assyria I have heard....

" 'The pride of Assyria shall be brought down, and the scepter of Egypt shall depart away.' Zechariah 10:11. This is true not only of the nations that arrayed themselves against God in ancient times, but also of nations today who fail of fulfilling the divine purpose. In the day of final awards, when the righteous Judge of all the earth shall 'sift the nations' (Isaiah 30:28), and those that have kept the truth shall be permitted to enter the City of God, heaven's arches will ring with the triumphant songs of the redeemed. 'Ye shall have a song,' the prophet declares, 'as in the night when a holy solemnity is kept; and gladness of heart, as when one goeth with a pipe to come into the mountain of the Lord, to the Mighty One of Israel. And the Lord shall cause His glorious voice to be heard....Through the voice of the Lord shall the Assyrian be beaten down, which smote with a rod" (*Prophets and Kings,* pp. 353-356, 359, 366).

- Chapter Seventy-four -

# How Nehemiah Prayed

***Read about Nehemiah***—"Their ideas of religious liberty are being woven with suggestions that do not come from the Holy Spirit, and the religious liberty cause is sickening, and its sickness can only be healed by the grace and gentleness of Christ.

"The hearts of those who advocate this cause must be filled by the spirit of Jesus. The Great Physician alone can apply the balm of Gilead. Let these men read the book of Nehemiah with humble hearts touched by the Holy Spirit. and their false ideas will be modified, and correct principles will be seen, and the present order of things will be changed. Nehemiah prayed to God for help, and God heard his prayer. The Lord moved upon heathen kings to come to his help. When his enemies zealously worked against him, the Lord worked through kings to carry out His purpose, and to answer the many prayers that were ascending to Him for help which they so much needed" (*Testimonies to Ministers and Gospel Workers,* pp. 200, 201).

*The kind of men God can use*—"God demonstrated to the people for whom He had done so much that He would not serve with their sins. He wrought, not through those who refused to serve Him with singleness of purpose, who had corrupted their ways before Him, but through Nehemiah; for he was registered in the books of heaven as a man. God has said, 'Them that honor me I will honor.' Nehemiah showed himself to be a man whom God could use to put down false principles and to restore heaven-born principles; and God honored him. The Lord will use in His work men who are as true as steel to principle, who will not be swayed by the sophistries of those who have lost their spiritual eyesight.

"Nehemiah was chosen by God because he was willing to cooperate with the Lord as a restorer. Falsehood and intrigue were used to pervert his integrity, but he would not be bribed. He refused to be corrupted by the devices of unprincipled men, who had been hired to do an evil work. He would not allow them to intimidate him into following a cowardly course. When he saw wrong principles being acted upon, he did not stand by as an onlooker, and by his silence give consent. He did not leave the people to conclude that he was standing on the wrong side. He took a firm, unyielding stand for the right. He would not lend one jot of influence to the perversion of the principles that God has established. Whatever the course others might pursue, he could say, 'So did not I, because of the fear of God.'

"In his work, Nehemiah kept the honor and glory of God ever in view. The governors that had been before him had dealt unjustly with the people, 'and had taken of them bread and wine, beside forty shekels of silver; yea, even their servants bear rule over the people.' 'But so did not I,' Nehemiah declared, 'because of the fear of God'" (*S.D.A. Bible Commentary*, vol. 3, pp. 1135, 1136; *The Review and Herald*, May 2, 1899).

*Prayer brought courage*—"By messengers from Judea the Hebrew patriot learned that days of trial had come to Jerusalem, the chosen city. The returned exiles were suffering affliction and reproach. The temple and portions of the city had been rebuilt; but the work of restoration was hindered, the temple services were disturbed, and the people kept in constant alarm by the fact that the walls of the city were still largely in ruins.

"Overwhelmed with sorrow, Nehemiah could neither eat nor drink; he 'wept, and mourned certain days, and fasted.' In his grief he turned to the divine Helper. 'I... prayed,' he said, 'before the God of heaven.' Faithfully he made confession of his sins and the sins of his people. He pleaded that God would maintain the cause of Israel, restore their courage and strength, and help them to build up the waste places of Judah.

"As Nehemiah prayed, his faith and courage grew strong. His mouth was filled with holy arguments. He pointed to the dishonor that would be cast upon God, if His people, now that they had returned to Him, should be left in weakness and oppression; and he urged the Lord to bring to pass His promise: 'If ye turn unto Me, and keep My commandments, and do them; though there were of you cast unto the uttermost part of the heaven, yet will I gather them from thence, and will bring them unto the place that I have chosen to set My name there.' See Deuteronomy 4:29-31. This promise had been given to Israel through Moses before they had entered Canaan, and during the centuries it had stood unchanged. God's people had now returned to Him in penitence and faith, and His promise would not fail.

"Nehemiah had often poured out his soul in behalf of his people. But now as he prayed a holy purpose formed in his mind. He resolved that if he could obtain the consent of the king, and the necessary aid in procuring implements and material, he would himself undertake the task of rebuilding the walls of Jerusalem and restoring Israel's national strength. And he asked the Lord to grant him favor in the sight of the king, that this plan might be carried out. 'Prosper, I pray Thee, Thy servant this day,' he entreated, 'and grant him mercy in the sight of this man.'

"Four months Nehemiah waited for a favorable opportunity to present his request to the king" (*Prophets and Kings,* pp. 628-630).

***Study the prayer***—[Nehemiah 1:5, 6 quoted.] "Not only did Nehemiah say that Israel had sinned. He acknowledged with penitence that he and his father's house had sinned. 'We have dealt corruptly against Thee,' he says, placing himself among those who had dishonored God by not standing stiffly for the truth....

"Nehemiah humbled himself before God, giving Him the glory due unto His name. Thus also did Daniel in Babylon. Let us study the prayers of these men. They teach us that we are to humble ourselves, but that we are never to obliterate the line of demarcation between God's commandment-keeping people and those who have no respect for His law.

"We all need to draw near to God. He will draw near to those who approach Him in humility, filled with holy awe for His sacred majesty, and standing before Him separate from the world" (*S.D.A. Bible Commentary,* vol. 3, p. 1136; Ms. 58, 1903).

**Taking hold of the promise**—"By faith taking fast hold of the divine promise, Nehemiah laid down at the footstool of heavenly mercy his petition that God would maintain the cause of His penitent people, restore their strength, and build up their waste places. God had been faithful to His threatenings when His people separated from Him; He had scattered them abroad among the nations, according to His Word. And Nehemiah found in this very fact an assurance that He would be equally faithful in fulfilling His promises" (*S.D.A. Bible Commentary*, vol. 3, p. 1136; *The Southern Watchman*, Mar. 1, 1904).

**Darted up a prayer**—"At length the sorrow that burdened the patriot's heart could no longer be concealed. Sleepless nights and care-filled days left their trace upon his countenance. The king, jealous for his own safety, was accustomed to read countenances and to penetrate disguises, and he saw that some secret trouble was preying upon his cupbearer. 'Why is thy countenance sad,' he inquired, 'seeing thou art not sick? this is nothing else but sorrow of heart.'

"The question filled Nehemiah with apprehension. Would not the king be angry to hear that while outwardly engaged in his service, the courtier's thoughts had been far away with his afflicted people? Would not the offender's life be forfeited? His cherished plan for restoring the strength of Jerusalem was it about to be overthrown? 'Then,' he writes, 'I was very sore afraid.' With trembling lips and tearful eyes he revealed the cause of his sorrow. 'Let the king live forever,' He answered. 'Why should not my countenance be sad, when the city, the place of my fathers' sepulchers, lieth waste, and the gates thereof are consumed with fire?'

"The recital of the condition of Jerusalem awakened the sympathy of the monarch without arousing his prejudices. Another question gave the opportunity for which Nehemiah had long waited: 'For what dost thou make request?' But the man of God did not venture to reply till he had sought direction from One higher than Artaxerxes. He had a sacred trust to fulfill, in which he required help from the king; and he realized that much depended upon his presenting the matter in such a way as to win his approval and enlist his aid. 'I prayed,' he said, 'to the God of heaven.' In that brief prayer Nehemiah pressed into the presence of the King of kings and won to his side a power that can turn hearts as the rivers of waters are turned" (*Prophets and Kings,* pp. 630, 631).

**Wherever we are**—"God in His providence does not permit us to know the end from the beginning; but He gives us the light of His Word to guide us as we pass along, and bids us to keep our minds stayed upon Jesus. Wherever we are, whatever our employment, our hearts are to be uplifted to God in prayer. This is being instant in prayer. We need not wait until we can bow upon our knees, before we pray. On one occasion, when Nehemiah came in before the king, the king asked why he looked so sad, and what request he had to make. But Nehemiah dared not answer at once. Important interests were at stake. The fate of a nation hung upon the impression that should then be made upon the monarch's mind; and Nehemiah darted up a prayer to the God of heaven, before he dared to answer the king. The result was that he obtained all that he asked or even desired" (*S.D.A. Bible Commentary*, vol. 3, p. 1136; *Historical Sketches of the Foreign Missions of the Seventh-day Adventists*, p. 144).

*Needed today*—"There is need of Nehemiahs in the church today, not men who can pray and preach only, but men whose prayers and sermons are braced with firm and eager purpose" (*S.D.A. Bible Commentary*, vol. 3, p. 1137; *The Southern Watchman*, Mar. 29, 1904).

*A ready resource*—"To pray as Nehemiah prayed in his hour of need is a resource at the command of the Christian under circumstances when other forms of prayer may be impossible. Toilers in the busy walks of life, crowded and almost overwhelmed with perplexity, can send up a petition to God for divine guidance. Travelers by sea and land, when threatened with some great danger, can thus commit themselves to Heaven's protection. In times of sudden difficulty or peril the heart may send up its cry for help to One who has pledged Himself to come to the aid of His faithful, believing ones whenever they call upon Him. In every circumstance, under every condition, the soul weighed down with grief and care, or fiercely assailed by temptation, may find assurance, support, and succor in the unfailing love and power of a covenant-keeping God.

"Nehemiah, in that brief moment of prayer to the King of kings, gathered courage to tell Artaxerxes of his desire to be released for a time from his duties at the court, and he asked for authority to build up the waste places of Jerusalem and to make it once more a strong and defensed city. Momentous results to the Jewish nation hung upon this request. 'And,' Nehemiah declares, 'the king granted me, according to the good hand of my God upon me'" (*Prophets and Kings*, pp. 631-633).

*Prayers continually going up*—"There is no time or place in which it is inappropriate to offer up a petition to God. There is nothing that can prevent us from lifting up our hearts in the spirit of earnest prayer. In the crowds of the street, in the midst of a business engagement, we may send up a petition to God and plead for divine guidance, as did Nehemiah when he made his request before King Artaxerxes. A closet of communion may be found wherever we are. We should have the door of the heart open continually and our invitation going up that Jesus may come and abide as a heavenly guest in the soul" (*Steps to Christ*, p. 99).

***Upon reaching Jerusalem***—"In secrecy and silence Nehemiah completed his circuit of the walls. 'The rulers knew not whither I went,' he declares, 'or what I did; neither had I as yet told it to the Jews, nor to the priests, nor to the nobles, nor to the rulers, nor to the rest that did the work.' The remainder of the night he spent in prayer; for he knew that the morning would call for earnest effort to arouse and unite his dispirited and divided countrymen" (*Prophets and Kings,* pp. 636, 637).

***Only with prayer did the work continue***—"How much anguish of soul this needed severity cost the faithful worker for God the judgment alone will reveal. There was a constant struggle with opposing elements, and only by fasting, humiliation, and prayer was advancement made....

"In the work of reform to be carried forward today, there is need of men who, like Ezra and Nehemiah, will not palliate or excuse sin, nor shrink from vindicating the honor of God. Those upon whom rests the burden of this work will not hold their peace when wrong is done, neither will they cover evil with a cloak of false charity. They will remember that God is no respecter of persons, and that severity to a few may prove mercy to many. They will remember also that in the one who rebukes evil the spirit of Christ should ever be revealed.

"In their work, Ezra and Nehemiah humbled themselves before God, confessing their sins and the sins of their people, and entreating pardon as if they themselves were the offenders. Patiently they toiled and prayed and suffered. That which made their work most difficult was not the open hostility of the heathen, but the secret opposition of pretended friends, who, by lending their influence to the service of evil, increased tenfold the burden of God's servants. These traitors furnished the Lord's enemies with material to use in their warfare upon His people. Their evil passions and rebellious wills were ever at war with the plain requirements of God.

"The success attending Nehemiah's efforts shows what prayer, faith, and wise energetic action will accomplish. Nehemiah was not a priest; he was not a prophet; he made no pretension to high title. He was a reformer raised up for an important time. It was his aim to set his people right with God. Inspired with a great purpose, he bent every energy of his being to its accomplishment. High, unbending integrity marked his efforts. As he came into contact with evil and opposition to right he took so determined a stand that the people were roused to labor with fresh zeal and courage. They could not but recognize his loyalty, his patriotism, and his deep love for God; and, seeing this, they were willing to follow where he led" (*Prophets and Kings,* pp. 674-676).

*- Chapter Seventy-five -*

# How John the Baptist Prayed

**Should be our experience**—"The experience of Enoch and of John the Baptist represents what ours should be. Far more than we do, we need to study the lives of these men he who was translated to heaven without seeing death, and he who, before Christ's first advent, was called to prepare the way of the Lord, to make His paths straight" (*Testimonies for the Church*, vol. 8, p. 329).

**Preparation for service**—"The life of John was not spent in idleness, in ascetic gloom, or in selfish isolation. From time to time he went forth to mingle with men; and he was ever an interested observer of what was passing in the world. From his quiet retreat he watched the unfolding of events. The burden of his mission was upon him. In solitude, by meditation and prayer, he sought to gird up his soul for the lifework before him" (*Gospel Workers,* p. 57).

**Christ was his study**—"John the Baptist in his desert life was taught of God. He studied the revelations of God in nature. Under the guiding of the Divine Spirit, he studied the scrolls of the prophets. By day and by night, Christ was his study, his meditation, until mind and heart and soul were filled with the glorious vision" (*Testimonies for the Church*, vol. 8, p. 331).

**Results of spiritual vision**—"He looked upon the King in His beauty, and self was lost sight of. He beheld the majesty of holiness and knew himself to be inefficient and unworthy. It was God's message that he was to declare. It was in God's power and His righteousness that he was to stand. He was ready to go forth as Heaven's messenger, un-awed by the human, because he had looked upon the Divine. He could stand fearless in the presence of earthly monarchs because with trembling he had bowed before the King of kings. With no elaborate arguments or finespun theories did John declare his message" (*Testimonies for the Church*, vol. 8, pp. 331, 332).

**Vision produced humility**—"Looking in faith to the Redeemer, John had risen to the height of self-abnegation. He sought not to attract men to himself, but to lift their thoughts higher and still higher, until they should rest upon the Lamb of God. He himself had been only a voice, a cry in the wilderness" (*Testimonies for the Church*, vol. 8, p. 333).

"The soul of the prophet, emptied of self, was filled with the light of the Divine" (*Testimonies for the Church*, vol. 8, p. 334).

*Ours a similar message*—"In this age, just prior to the second coming of Christ in the clouds of heaven, such a work as that of John is to be done" (*Testimonies for the Church*, vol. 8, p. 332).

"In order to give such a message as John gave, we must have a spiritual experience like his. The same work must be wrought in us. We must behold God, and in beholding Him lose sight of self

"John had by nature the faults and weaknesses common to humanity; but the touch of divine love had transformed him" (*Testimonies for the Church*, vol. 8, p. 333).

*- Chapter Seventy-six -*

# How Martin Luther Prayed

*The pleading of Martin Luther*—"The next day he was to appear to render his final answer. For a time his heart sank within him as he contemplated the forces that were combined against the truth. His faith faltered; fearfulness and trembling came upon him, and horror overwhelmed him. Dangers multiplied before him; his enemies seemed about to triumph, and the powers of darkness to prevail. Clouds gathered about him and seemed to separate him from God. He longed for the assurance that the Lord of hosts was with him. In anguish of spirit he threw himself with his face upon the earth and poured out those broken, heart-rending cries, which none but God can fully understand.

"'O almighty and everlasting God,' he pleaded, 'how terrible is this world! Behold, it openeth its mouth to swallow me up, and I have so little trust in Thee.... If it is only in the strength of this world that I must put my trust, all is over....My last hour is come, my condemnation has been pronounced....O God, do Thou help me against all the wisdom of the world. Do this,...Thou alone;...for this is not my work, but Thine. I have nothing to do here, nothing to contend for with these great ones of the world....But the cause is Thine,...and it is a righteous and eternal cause. O Lord, help me! Faithful and unchangeable God, in no man do I place my trust....All that is of man is uncertain; all that cometh of man fails....Thou hast chosen me for this work.... Stand at my side, for the sake of Thy well-beloved Jesus Christ, who is my defense, my shield, and my strong tower.'

"An all-wise Providence had permitted Luther to realize his peril, that he might not trust in his own strength and rush presumptuously into danger. Yet it was not the fear of personal suffering, a dread of torture or death, which seemed immediately impending, that overwhelmed him with its terror. He had come to the crisis, and he felt his insufficiency to meet it. Through his weakness the cause of truth might suffer loss. Not for his own safety, but for the triumph of the gospel did he wrestle with God. Like Israel's, in that night struggle beside the lonely stream, was the anguish and conflict of his soul. Like Israel, he prevailed with God. In his utter helplessness his faith fastened upon Christ, the mighty Deliverer. He was strengthened with the assurance that he would not appear alone before the council. Peace returned to his soul, and he rejoiced that he was permitted to uplift the word of God before the rulers of the nations.

"With his mind stayed upon God, Luther prepared for the struggle before him. He thought upon the plan of his answer, examined passages in his own writings, and drew from the Holy Scriptures suitable proofs to sustain his positions. Then, laying his left hand on the Sacred Volume, which was open before him, he lifted his right hand to heaven and vowed 'to remain faithful to the gospel, and freely to confess his faith, even should he seal his testimony with his blood'" (*The Great Controversy,* pp. 156-158).

*The power that shook the world*—"When powerful foes were uniting to overthrow the reformed faith, and thousands of swords seemed about to be unsheathed against it, Luther wrote: 'Satan is putting forth his fury; ungodly pontiffs are conspiring; and we are threatened with war. Exhort the people to contend valiantly before the throne of the Lord, by faith and prayer, so that our enemies, vanquished by the Spirit of God, may be constrained to peace. Our chief want, our chief labor, is prayer; let the people know that they are now exposed to the edge of the sword and to the rage of Satan, and let them pray....

"From the secret place of prayer came the power that shook the world in the Great Reformation. There, with holy calmness, the servants of the Lord set their feet upon the rock of His promises. During the struggle at Augsburg, Luther 'did not pass a day without devoting three hours at least to prayer, and they were hours selected from those the most favorable to study.' In the privacy of his chamber he was heard to pour out his soul before God in words 'full of adoration, fear, and hope, as when one speaks to a friend.' 'I know that Thou art our Father and our God,' he said, 'and that Thou wilt scatter the persecutors of Thy children; for Thou art Thyself endangered with us. All this matter is Thine, and it is only by Thy constraint that we have put our hands to do it. Defend us, then, O Father!'

"To Melanchthon, who was crushed under the burden of anxiety and fear, he wrote: 'Grace and peace in Christ in Christ, I say, and not in the world. Amen. I hate with exceeding hatred those extreme cares which consume you. If the cause is unjust, abandon it; if the cause is just, why should we belie the promises of Him who commands us to sleep without fear?...Christ will not be wanting to the work of justice and truth. He lives, He reigns; what fear, then, can we have?'" (*The Great Controversy,* pp. 209, 210).

# Chapter Seventy-seven

# How Jesus Prayed - 1

**From hours spent with God**—"Not for Himself, but for others, He lived and thought and prayed. From hours spent with God he came forth morning by morning, to bring the light of heaven to men. Daily He received a fresh baptism of the Holy Spirit. In the early hours of the new day the Lord awakened Him from His slumbers, and His soul and His lips were anointed with grace, that He might impart to others. His words were given Him fresh from the heavenly courts, words that He might speak in season to the weary and oppressed. 'The Lord God hath given Me,' He said, 'the tongue of the learned, that I should know how to speak a word in season to him that is weary: He wakeneth morning by morning, He wakeneth Mine ear to hear as the learned.' Isaiah 50:4.

"Christ's disciples were much impressed by His prayers and by His habit of communion with God. One day after a short absence from their Lord, they found Him absorbed in supplication. Seeming unconscious of their presence, He continued praying aloud. The hearts of the disciples were deeply moved. As He ceased praying, they exclaimed, 'Lord, teach us to pray'" (*Christ's Object Lessons*, pp. 139, 140).

**Strengthened for duties and trial**—"As the human was upon Him, He felt His need of strength from His Father. He had select places of prayer. He loved to hold communion with His Father in the solitude of the mountain. In this exercise His holy, human soul was strengthened for the duties and trials of the day. Our Saviour identifies Himself with our needs and weaknesses, in that He became a suppliant, a nightly petitioner, seeking from His Father fresh supplies of strength, to come forth invigorated and refreshed, braced for duty and trial. He is our example in all things" (*Testimonies for the Church*, vol. 2, pp. 201, 202).

**Continual prayer**—"It was not on the cross only that Christ sacrificed Himself for humanity. As He 'went about doing good' (Acts 10:38), every day's experience was an outpouring of His life. In one way only could such a life be sustained. Jesus lived in dependence upon God and communion with Him. To the secret place of the Most High, under the shadow of the Almighty, men now and then repair; they abide for a season, and the result is manifest in noble deeds; then their faith fails, the communion is interrupted, and lifework marred. But the life of Jesus was a life of constant trust, sustained by continual communion; and His service for heaven and earth was without failure or faltering.

"As a man He supplicated the throne of God, till His humanity was charged with

159

a heavenly current that connected humanity with divinity. Receiving life from God, He imparted life to men" (*Education,* pp. 80, 81).

**His hours of happiness**—"He studied the word of God, and His hours of greatest happiness were found when He could turn aside from the scene of His labors to go into the fields, to meditate in the quiet valleys, to hold communion with God on the mountainside or amid the trees of the forest. The early morning often found Him in some secluded place, meditating, searching the Scriptures, or in prayer. With the voice of singing He welcomed the morning light. With songs of thanksgiving He cheered His hours of labor and brought heaven's gladness to the toilworn and disheartened" (*The Ministry of Healing,* p. 52).

**Alone with God**—"In a life wholly devoted to the good of others, the Saviour found it necessary to turn aside from ceaseless activity and contact with human needs, to seek retirement and unbroken communion with His Father. As the throng that had followed Him depart, He goes into the mountains, and there, alone with God, pours out His soul in prayer for these suffering, sinful, needy ones" (*The Ministry of Healing,* p. 58).

**Few follow His example**—"Few are willing to imitate His amazing privations, to endure His sufferings and persecutions, and to share His exhausting labor to bring others to the light. But few will follow His example in earnest, frequent prayer to God for strength to endure the trials of this lift and perform its daily duties. Christ is the Captain of our salvation, and by His own sufferings and sacrifice He has given an example to all His followers that watchfulness and prayer, and persevering effort, were necessary on their part if they would rightly represent the love which dwelt in His bosom for the fallen race" (*Testimonies for the Church,* vol. 2, p. 664).

*- Chapter Seventy-eight -*

# How Jesus Prayed - 2

**A necessity**—"Jesus Himself, while He dwelt among men, was often in prayer. Our Saviour identified Himself with our needs and weaknesses, in that He became suppliant, a petitioner, seeking from His Father fresh supplies of strength, that He might come forth braced for duty and trial. He is our example in all things. He is a brother in our infirmities, 'in all points tempted like as we are;' but as the sinless one

His nature recoiled from evil; He endured struggles and torture of soul in a world of sin. His humanity made prayer a necessity and a privilege. He found comfort and joy in communion with His Father. And if the Saviour of men, the Son of God, felt the need of prayer, how much more should feeble, sinful mortals feel the necessity of fervent, constant prayer" (*Steps to Christ,* pp. 93, 94).

**Bent in prayer**—"Christ gave no stinted service. He did not measure His work by hours. His time, His heart, His soul and strength, were given to labor for the benefit of humanity. Through weary days He toiled, and through long nights He bent in prayer for grace and endurance that He might do a larger work. With strong crying and tears He sent His petitions to heaven, that His human nature might be strengthened, that He might be braced to meet the wily foe in all his deceptive workings, and fortified to fulfill His mission of uplifting humanity. To His workers He says, 'I have given you an example, that ye should do as I have done.' John 13:15" (*The Ministry of Healing,* p. 500).

**Knelt in prayer**—"Both in public and in private worship, it is our privilege to bow on our knees before the Lord when we offer our petitions to Him. Jesus, our example, 'kneeled down, and prayed'" (*Gospel Workers*, p. 178).

**Secret of power**—"The Saviour's life on earth was a life of communion with nature and with God. In this communion He revealed for us the secret of a life of power" (*The Ministry of Healing,* p. 51).

**His experience is to be ours**—"In a life wholly devoted to the good of others, the Saviour found it necessary to withdraw from the thoroughfares of travel and from the throng that followed Him day after day. He must turn aside from a life of ceaseless activity and contact with human needs, to seek retirement and unbroken communion with His Father. As one with us, a sharer in our needs and weaknesses, He was wholly dependent upon God, and in the secret place of prayer He sought divine strength, that He might go forth braced for duty and trial. In a world of sin Jesus endured struggles and torture of soul. In communion with God He could unburden the sorrows that were crushing Him. Here He found comfort and joy.

"In Christ the cry of humanity reached the Father of infinite pity. As a man He supplicated the throne of God till His humanity was charged with a heavenly current that should connect humanity with divinity. Through continual communion He received life from God, that He might impart life to the world. His experience is to be ours" (*The Desire of Ages,* pp. 362, 363).

*With strong crying and tears*—"The man of Sorrows pours out His supplications with strong crying and tears. He prays for strength to endure the test in behalf of humanity. He must Himself gain a fresh hold on Omnipotence, for only thus can He contemplate the future. And He pours out His heart longings for His disciples, that in the hour of the power of darkness their faith may not fail. The dew is heavy upon His bowed form, but He heeds it not. The shadows of night gather thickly about Him, but He regards not their gloom. So the hours pass slowly by" (*The Desire of Ages,* pp. 419, 420).

*Strengthened faith by prayer*—"To the consecrated worker there is wonderful consolation in the knowledge that even Christ during His life on earth sought His Father daily for fresh supplies of needed grace; and from this communion with God He went forth to strengthen and bless others. Behold the Son of God bowed in prayer to His Father! Though He is the Son of God, He strengthens His faith by prayer, and by communion with heaven gathers to Himself power to resist evil and to minister to the needs of men. As the Elder Brother of our race He knows the necessities of those who, compassed with infirmity and living in a world of sin and temptation, still desire to serve Him. He knows that the messengers whom He sees fit to send are weak, erring men; but to all who give themselves wholly to His service He promises divine aid. His own example is an assurance that earnest, persevering supplication to God in faith faith that leads to entire dependence upon God, and unreserved consecration to His work will avail to bring to men the Holy Spirit's aid in the battle against sin" (*The Acts of the Apostles,* p. 56).

*Christ reveals to angels His coming agony*—"He then made known to the angelic host that a way of escape had been made for lost man....[He told them] that He would suffer dreadful hours of agony, which even angels could not look upon, but would veil their faces from the sight. Not merely agony of body would He suffer, but mental agony, that with which bodily suffering could in no wise be compared. The weight of the sins of the whole world would be upon Him" (*Early Writings*, pp. 149, 150).

*Christ's earthly suffering in the wilderness*—"When Jesus entered the wilderness, He was shut in by the Father's glory....But the glory departed, and He was left to battle with temptation. It was pressing upon Him every moment. His human nature shrank from the conflict that awaited Him. For forty days He fasted and prayed. Weak and emaciated from hunger, worn and haggard with mental agony, 'His visage was so marred more than any man, and His form more than the sons of men'" (*The Desire of Ages,* p. 118).

***His suffering in Gethsemane***—"Behold Him contemplating the price to be paid for the human soul. In His agony He clings to the cold ground, as if to prevent Himself from being drawn farther from God" (*The Desire of Ages,* p. 687).

***The Christian is to pray with great earnestness and sincerity***—"Be in earnest, be sincere. Fervent prayer availeth much. Jacob-like, wrestle in prayer. Agonize. Jesus, in the garden, sweat great drops of blood; you must make an effort" (*Testimonies for the Church,* vol. 1, p. 158).

***Agonizing without the surrender of self is useless***—"There are many souls who wrestle for special victories and special blessings that they may do some great thing. To this end they are always feeling that they must make an agonizing struggle in prayer and tears....All the agonizing, all the tears and struggles, will not bring them the blessing they long for. Self must be entirely surrendered" (*Testimonies for the Church*, vol. 9, p. 165).

(For more on the actual prayers of Christ, read *The Desire of Ages*, pp. 111-113, 379, 420-421, 680, 687-693, 744-745, 760; *The Acts of the Apostles*, pp. 20, 21; *Thoughts from the Mount of Blessing*, p. 103; *Selected Messages*, book 1, p. 167; *Testimonies for the Church*, vol. 2, pp. 208, 209; *Testimonies for the Church*, vol. 4, pp. 529, 530; *My Life Today,* p. 252.)

- *Chapter Seventy-nine* -

# *Joshua and the Angel*

***The pleading of Joshua***—The vision that Zechariah had of Joshua standing before God as he pled for himself and his people is a prophecy that applies to God's faithful ones in these last days. Carefully read the inspired commentary on this Zechariah 3 passage. It is found in *Testimonies for the Church*, vol. 5, pp. 467-476. Read it several times, for it is deep with meaning. A parallel passage is *Testimonies for the Church*, vol. 5, pp. 212-216.

# Chapter Eighty

# Jacob's Trouble

*Jacob's wrestling and Jacob's trouble*—The experience that Jacob underwent as his brother came out to slay him and his loved ones, the prayer experience that night, the wrestling with the angel that climaxed it, and the deliverance that followed it, are all a type of the experience that the people of God will undergo between the close of human probation and their deliverance by the voice of God sounding from heaven. Many important principles are dealt with here, and they should be carefully studied. You will want to read the following passages: *Patriarchs and Prophets*, pp. 195-203; *The Great Controversy*, pp. 619-632; *The Story of Redemption*, pp. 94-99; *Spiritual Gifts*, vol. 3, pp. 128-137.

We invite you to view the complete
selection of titles we publish at:

**www.TEACHServices.com**

Scan with your mobile
device to go directly
to our website.

or write or email us your praises, reactions,
or thoughts about this or any other book we publish at:

# TEACH Services, Inc.
## P U B L I S H I N G
### *www.TEACHServices.com*

P.O. Box 954
Ringgold, GA 30736

**info@TEACHServices.com**

TEACH Services, Inc., titles may be purchased in bulk for
educational, business, fund-raising, or sales promotional use.
For information, please e-mail:

**BulkSales@TEACHServices.com**

Finally, if you are interested in seeing
your own book in print, please contact us at

**publishing@TEACHServices.com**

We would be happy to review your manuscript for free.

CPSIA information can be obtained
at www.ICGtesting.com
Printed in the USA
FSHW021630021120
75382FS